Table Decor

Festive Occasions, Weddings, & Other Special Events

E. Ashley Rooney

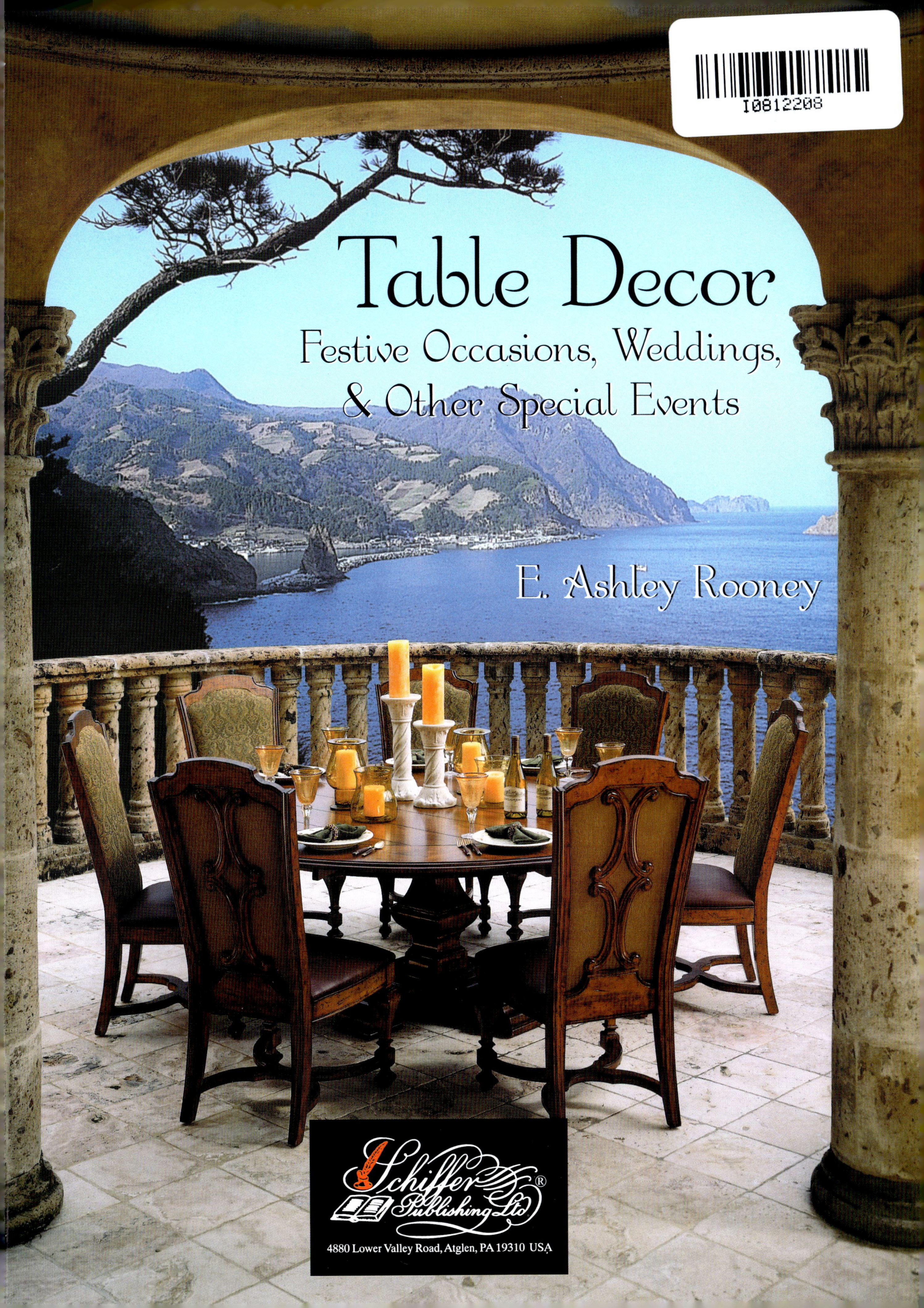

Schiffer Publishing Ltd®
4880 Lower Valley Road, Atglen, PA 19310 USA

Other Schiffer Books by E. Ashley Rooney:
Waterfront Homes: from Castles to Cottages (2003)
Garden Ornaments: Pots, Pergolas, Pedestals and More (2003)
Old Barns – New Homes: A Showcase of Architectural Conversions (2004)
Spectacular Small Kitchens: Design Ideas for Urban Spaces (2005)
Retreats to Retirement: Dreams to Reality (2005)
Cliffhangers and Hillside Houses (2006)

Other Schiffer Books on Related Subjects:
Food Art: Garnishing Made Easy John Gargone
Tea & Taste: The Visual Language of Tea Tania M. Buckrell Pos
The Bridal Bouquet Book Ginny Parfitt
Yesterday's Silver for Today's Table Richard Osterberg

Acknowledgments

That Girl Scout song talks about making new friends while keeping the old. This book certainly brought new friends into my life. It was Tuulikki Loring, an innovative decorator, who said to me, "But you must get pictures of that teddybear tea!" She was right. And Tuulikki went on to design lovely whimsical tables for the book. Later, I got to know Christina Gamota, with her great sense of detail and knowledge of decor. She also designed many stunning tables for this book.

There were many others. The Lexington Field and Garden Club brought forth many wonderful representatives of its talent and skill. My friends and family opened their china closets, sideboards, and silver chests and shared their collectibles.

Then the wonderful cameras of my husband D. Peter Lund, Paul Doherty, Siobhan Theriault, and Knut Wefald went to work and, voila! The book took off.

Photography by D. Peter Lund, unless otherwise credited
Front Cover: *Courtesy of Kate Dickerson Design, Inc. and Martin's Herend Imports, Inc.*
Spine: *Courtesy of Kate Dickerson Design, Inc.*
Back Cover: *Courtesy of Martin's Herend Imports, Inc.*
Title Page: *Courtesy of Stanley Furniture Company*

Library of Congress Control Number: 2006927489

Designed by John P. Cheek
Cover design by Bruce Waters
Type set in Seagull Hv BT/Aldine 721 BT

ISBN: 0-7643-2472-1
Printed in China

Published by Schiffer Publishing Ltd.
4880 Lower Valley Road
Atglen, PA 19310
Phone: (610) 593-1777; Fax: (610) 593-2002
E-mail: Info@schifferbooks.com

For the largest selection of fine reference books on this and related subjects, please visit our web site at
www.schifferbooks.com
We are always looking for people to write books on new and related subjects. If you have an idea for a book please contact us at the above address.

This book may be purchased from the publisher.
Include $3.95 for shipping.
Please try your bookstore first.
You may write for a free catalog.

In Europe, Schiffer books are distributed by
Bushwood Books
6 Marksbury Ave.
Kew Gardens
Surrey TW9 4JF England
Phone: 44 (0) 20 8392-8585;
Fax: 44 (0) 20 8392-9876
E-mail: info@bushwoodbooks.co.uk
Website: www.bushwoodbooks.co.uk
Free postage in the U.K., Europe; air mail at cost.

Contents

Foreword

Mary Lou Touart

Some hostesses, with unlimited means, often hire professional decorators to create table settings for their special parties when the occasion demands it. Such a specialist will talk to you about the event you wish to give and what impression you want to create.

But you can do the same thing if you look around your house or apartment. See what you have that's interesting and unusual to create your own imaginative table settings and please everyone who attends. If you like to entertain, start collecting varieties of china, pottery, glassware, and enticing table ornaments, as well as linens of all colors and designs. Select them as though you were planning a coordinated wardrobe and enjoy playing the "mix and match" game.

When planning formal dinners, start with the dishes. Get out your grandmothers' Limoges, Spode, or Haviland dinnerware, her crystal goblets, the heavy linen table cloth and big square matching napkins, hand-embroidered with the family monogram. Consider the silver candlesticks or the crystal ones. Use the family silver flatware. Try using other small china or crystal animals or dishes. Then go all out with colorful candles, an extravagant bouquet of unusual flowers (calla lilies, orchids, anemones, or old fashioned roses). You might consider copying the Japanese Ikebana idea that uses few flowers to great effect.

Brilliant tablecloths in purple, scarlet, or deep turquoise can set off the glow of the porcelain and crystal for a sophisticated presentation. This is a truly formal setting for a very special occasion. It also needs special food and wines: oysters Rockefeller, a standing rib roast or lobster Newburg, intriguing vegetables, and a flaming dessert with a dessert wine as the classic finale.

Other formal occasions on a sunny summer terrace or porch, such as intimate lunches with special friends, a bridal shower, or an anniversary party, can be addressed in the same colorful, formal ways. Here is where flowers and lovely linens, plus chargers and plates in different patterns, can come into play. Plants and flowers in similar hues, on the floor of a terrace or porch, can enhance the festivities. Don't forget candles if it's twilight and beyond, plus lighted torchéres. This setting makes for a sultry and romantic evening.

Sturdy pottery is more ethnic and informal in feeling. It could be Mexican, Japanese, Italian, French, or even southwest USA. Here is where color, and lots of it, can play a big part. Prints can appear on napkins and/or tablecloths. Think about covering your table with a paisley shawl, a printed sheet, or a length of batik. You could also use bandanas for napkins. Extravagant centerpieces, with flowers and foliage or fruits, vegetables, and sheaves of wheat, could serve nicely. Candles of all shapes and sizes add allure to such a setting, particularly one that is outdoors, in the garden, or on a patio.

If you have a theme (Colorado ranch, Atlantic sailing, New England clambake, or southern), carry it throughout.

- At the entry, set up a bar on a card table covered with a bright cloth.
- See that the glasses are marked by an identifying color for each guest.
- Color your ice cubes with vegetable dyes.
- Post a drink list: metropolitans, apple martinis, gin and tonics, piña coladas, or even Mexican beer, whatever!
- Have a selection of simple before-dinner snacks. Popcorn, blue corn chips and cheese sticks are all tasty and easy to eat.
- This is the time to show off your barbecue skills with grilled veggies. Corn on the cob and plates of ripe tomatoes sprinkled with fresh dill are just the right accompaniments.
- Then have watermelon for dessert.

With this kind of attention to detail, using color, delicious food, and a charming table setting, your guests — even the least visual of them — will enjoy both the food and the company more, without quite knowing why!

Eat cheese with a fork, not a knife.

Never put your own knife, fork or spoon into a dish from which others are to be helped.

Break your bread, do not cut it.

Eat fruit with silver knives and forks.

If you prefer, take up asparagus with the fingers. Olives and artichokes are always so eaten.

Use a napkin only for your mouth. Never use it for your nose, face or forehead.

It is very rude to pick your teeth at the table. If it becomes necessary to do so, hold your napkin over your mouth.

Rules of Etiquette and Home Culture, 1886

Courtesy of Martin's Herend Imports, Inc.

Courtesy of Siobhan Theriault

Courtesy of Martin's Herend Imports, Inc.

Courtesy of Grass Roots Florist

Courtesy of Siobhan Theriault

Courtesy of Grass Roots Florist

***Right:** Courtesy of Thomas Van Veen Photography for Elegance & Simplicity Wedding & Event Designers, Inc.*

Courtesy of George Gamota

Courtesy of Design Ideas, Ltd

Courtesy of Kate Dickerson Design, Inc.

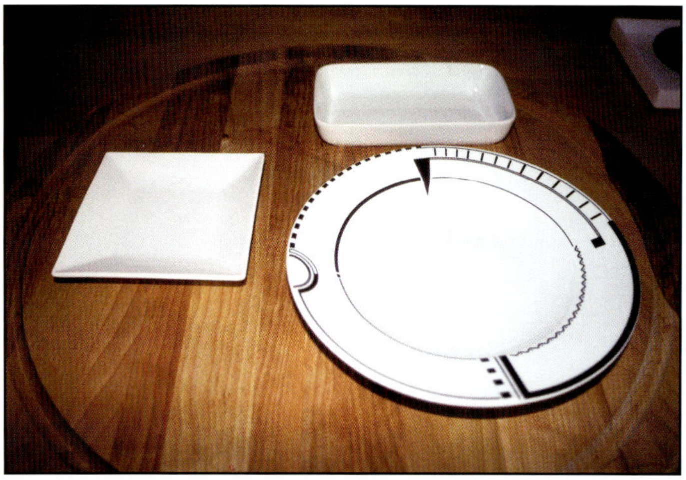

1. Short History of Table Setting

The table is the heart of the home. It is where we celebrate those significant occasions such as birthdays, anniversaries, and holidays. It is where we make memories. Today, many people agonize about the demise of the family's dinner hour. Meals can and should be a time when we break bread together; share our experiences, hopes, and dreams. Meals build community.

Setting the Table

Meals are governed by many rules. We learned, while young, that bones and fragments should be deposited quietly on the edge of our plate, for example. We should ask to be excused when leaving a table.

The primary rule for setting a dinner table is that the utensils should be geometrically spaced. All the seating places should be at equal distance, about two feet from the center of the next place (in other words, no elbows should touch), and all the flatware should be balanced.

A standard table setting consists of dishes, glassware, and cutlery for each course, with the cutting edges toward the plate. Forks are on the left and knives are on the right. The dessert spoon and fork are placed at the outer edges or at the top of the plate. If salad is served, it can be placed directly on the main course plate if the main course is cold. If the main course is hot, then the salad plate should be off to the side separately.

Generally, for a formal meal, one or two wines are served, so a water goblet and (one or two) wineglasses are necessary. When three glasses are used, they are usually placed in a triangle for a formal table setting, the water goblet closest to the dinner plate.

If coffee is to be served with the meal, the cup and saucer go to the right of the setting, with the coffee spoon resting on the right side of the saucer.

The rule is: liquids on the right, solids on the left. In other words, that's your coffee cup to the right of the plate and your bread plate on the left!

The history of table setting and table manners is extensive. Archeologists believe even cave dwellers offered food to strangers, hoping to demonstrate their peaceful intentions. Roman nobles dined from gold, silver, and pottery plates, while slaves ate from wooden bowls. When barbarians overran Europe, individual plates went out of general use.

In the Middle Ages, most people ate with their hands, using slices of stale bread known as *boules,* or "trenchers" to hold the food. *Boule,* which is French for ball, is bread made from whole wheat flour, rye, or barley baked as a round loaf. Once the *boule* was aged, it was sliced horizontally into rounds or rectangles (trenchers). Leftover trenchers were given to the poor – which is probably why teeth were scarce!

When people laid boards across trestles and covered them with cloth at mealtimes, they created the trestle table. After a meal, they dismantled the table and placed it at the side of the room where it was called a sideboard. This practice gives us the term "setting the table."

By the early 1500s, some enterprising believers in etiquette developed even more complex rules to govern eating behavior. No longer could you "blow your nose with the same hand that you use to hold the meat." Putting chewed bones back on your plate was forbidden. Instead, you were supposed to throw them on the floor for the dogs!

Forks, Knives, and Spoons

The Dutch humanist Erasmus pointed out, in his book of manners, *On Civility in Children*, that it was "a great breach of etiquette when your fingers are dirty and greasy, to bring them to your mouth in order to lick them, or to clean them on your jacket. It would be more decent to use the tablecloth."

In the Middle Ages, the noble men used their daggers or knives as utensils and cut the food for the women, when necessary. Sometimes, two knives were used—one to cut and the other to hold the meat in place. Knives also were used for a more murderous purpose. In 1669, King Louis XIV of France banned pointed knives from the dining table; blood shedding could wait until the meal was completed.

By the early eighteenth century, a four-tined fork had become standard in Europe. In England, though, forks generally had only two tines, which weren't very useful for picking up food. By the early nineteenth century, most people used tined forks or "split spoons."

With the introduction of the fork, rules governing table arrangements became more complicated. People customarily ate from plates and had their own cups. Bones were no longer thrown on the floor but were left on the plate. By the mid-nineteenth century, an almost mystifying assortment of cutlery, serving pieces, plates, and rules governed eating at a table. Spoons were individualized for use with food ranging from bouillon to demitasse to grapefruit. The wealthy housewife had a vast array of forks and knives for all sorts of specific food.

As tableware became more popular for a larger group of people, polite table practices became standardized. Forks were placed in their order of use, from the outside inward. Knives and spoons were positioned to the right of the plate. The bottom tips of all the flatware were aligned.

Today, table settings generally are simpler than in the past hundred years, but the rules are still there. When you know which utensils to use (and how to shed a fish bone), you are several steps ahead of the pack. Even in our relaxed society, table manners and well-set tables play a role in both making a favorable impression and a pleasant experience.

Courtesy of DeVine Corporation

Courtesy of Devine Corporation

> *We may never never meet again, on that bumpy road to love*
> *But I'll always, always keep the memory of*
> *The way you hold your knife*
> *The way we danced till three*
> *The way you changed my life*
> *No they can't take that away from me.*
> —Ira Gershwin, "They Can't Take That Away from Me."

Plates

François I of France, in 1536, initiated the use of a separate plate for each course.

Until the mid-nineteenth century, plates came in two sizes: large and medium, but the growing more affluent middle class wanted different plates for each specific food, such as dessert, fruit, and fish.

Today, plates are made in twelve different sizes for table use: service plate or charger, dinner, luncheon, round salad, crescent salad, fish, dessert, cheese, fruit, tea, bread and butter plate, and fruit saucer.

Bowls

Bowls come with and without handles to hold solid foods, contain soup, or (in my grandmother's time) to rinse the fingertips. To protect the table and balance the place setting, bowls are generally placed on an under plate – some even have specifically designed companion saucers.

The size and style of today's soup bowls are determined by the content's texture and temperature. Seven different shapes of soup bowls are available, ranging from wide shallow bowls for chunky soups, such as a borsht, to deep bowls for pureed soup.

Octagonal Chinese export cream soup plate, made for the English market, c. 1775.

> *"The soup had been put into three bowls—a great big bowl for the great big bear, a **medium-sized bowl** for the **medium-sized bear,** and a **teeny tiny bowl** for the **teeny tiny bear;** beside each bowl lay a spoon. Goldilocks took one and helped herself to a spoonful of soup from the great big bowl."*
> "Goldilocks and the Three Bears"

Coffee is served in the traditional Danish style on traditional Danish china.

Noritake is hard, white, translucent porcelain from Japan.

Cups

Until the seventeenth century, when the beverages coffee, tea, and hot chocolate were introduced, Europeans consumed cold beverages. When hot beverages were first available, they were consumed from handle-less bowls that were found in the crates of loose tea and used to measure the tea. Soon, Europeans began to make their own tea bowls. Tea was very expensive in the eighteenth century in Europe (it came from the Orient, a long distance away), and the early drinking bowls were only 2 or 3 ounces in size. Only wealthy consumers could afford Western-made handled cups. By the late eighteenth century, mass production manufacturing methods made handled cups affordable for the general public.

Today, cups are made in at least six sizes: breakfast, tea, coffee, chocolate, after dinner coffee, and demitasse cup. The strength of the drink, the hour it is served, and its viscosity determine the size.

Colorfully decorated with roosters in four different motifs, Chanticleer was introduced in the 1930s and modeled after a similar Herend pattern owned by Belgian royalty. *Courtesy of Martin's Herend Imports, Inc.*

> *"The morning cup of coffee has an exhilaration about it which the cheering influence of the afternoon or evening cup of tea cannot be expected to reproduce."*
> Oliver Wendell Holmes, Jr., *Over the Tea Cups*

Glasses

Even Pliny (23–79 A.D.) talks about wine glasses. When the Saxons invaded Europe, he recounts, they brought fine glassware, jewel-encrusted goblets, and drinking horns. The latter had no support, so when filled the contents had to be consumed before putting the vessel down; they were definitely for the original binge drinkers!

By the late 900s, wooden tankards were widespread in Europe. In the late 1000s, clear glass tumblers appeared. The mid-1300s introduced leather vessels or "black jacks" lined with pitch.

Around 1740, plain straight stems on wine glasses became fashionable. By the end of the eighteenth century, French glassblowers were producing crystal wine glasses. In the nineteenth century, Victorians delighted in a large assortment of different glasses. A dozen each of port, sherry, burgundy, claret, champagne, and liqueur glasses was not unusual in the middle-class pantry.

By the 1950s, glass stemware manufacturers had refined wine glass design so extensively that there was a unique size and shape for almost every type of wine available.

Rich with three centuries of tradition, the *cristalleries* of Portieux turn to the future. *Courtesy of DeVine Corporation*

A centuries-old wine glass is filled once again. *Courtesy of Siobhan Theriault*

In this era, when attention to detail makes a major difference, table settings play an important role.

A glass of champagne never goes out of style.

Servers

Banquets could have dozens of courses, in the eighteenth century, and a menu that required many different bowls, tureens, platters, etc. to serve them. In the early nineteenth century, dinner served *a la russe* became popular. This Russian style of service required a butler to present a platter at the banquet table and then return it to the kitchen for division onto individual dining plates, a practice which cut down on the number of required servers and staff.

Many historical styles were revived in the nineteenth century to enhance various decorating schemes. New serving pieces were designed for massive roasts, large fish, oysters, and dessert. Middle-class wives used compotes; oval, round, and shell-like bowls; epergnes; oval, rectangular, and even fish-shape platters; butter servers; gravy boats; jelly dishes; candy bowls; powdered sugar dispensers; biscuit boxes; pitchers; decanters—the list goes on.

From the seventeenth to the nineteenth centuries, formal meals in Europe and the Americas began with soup. Consequently, the large soup tureen, which is descended from a communal bowl, became fashionable as a practical vessel, table ornament, and symbol of prestige. Today, many elegant antique examples can be seen at the Winterthur Museum, in Delaware, which houses the Campbell Collection of soup tureens.

Of course, utensils for all the special servers were also compulsory for formal dining: ladles, spoons, forks, knives, tongs…

Hey diddle diddle, the cat and the fiddle,
The cow jumped over the moon,
The little dog laughed to see such sport,
And the dish ran away with the spoon.
—Old Mother Goose rhyme

Antique servers.

This intriguing item is an English biscuit box.

Handmade by a Thai craftsman, these bowls were made from large blocks of mango wood. *Courtesy of Design Ideas, Ltd.*

Table Linens

Boules (stale bread bowls) and salt cellars made up Middle Ages tables. Persons of distinction sat *above* the "saler" (salt cellar), which meant that they sat between it and the head of the table; dependents and inferior guests sat *below*. Guests ate with their fingers or carried their own utensils. They shared goblets that were placed on the sideboard.

Tablecloths

In the late sixteenth century, when the nobility began to use solid tables, tablecloths were used to cover the tables. Royalty used damask tablecloths that the Crusaders had introduced; damask was a princely material woven in Damascus with characteristic floral motifs or designs.

Tablecloths were used on both their top and under sides, a practical custom given the lack of washing facilities. A wrongdoer at that time was not allowed to eat from the same tablecloth as his peers; hence the expression, "he and I are not of the same cloth."

Luminex is an optical-sparkling fabric that emits its own light. This tablecloth radiates the joy of the occasion. *Courtesy of Luminex*

By the end of the eighteenth century, many textile mills were mass-producing cotton fabric; eventually, machine-made tablecloths were sold. Today, table linens are decorative accessories that visually bring the components on a table together, insulate the table from heat and scuffing of the plates, and reduce the noise level at the meal.

This modern-day cotton placemat magnifies the intricate pattern and texture of a single leaf, to yield a place setting worthy of table conversation. *Courtesy of Design Ideas, Ltd.*

Rudolph's unpretentious younger cousin wears a natty scarf and leads his own band of adolescent reindeer. *Courtesy of Design Ideas, Ltd.*

This exquisite, handmade lace mat and matching napkin have lasted for generations.

Napkins

In the early Middle Ages, people wiped their hands and mouths on the backs of their hands, on clothing, or on a piece of bread. Later, a napkin became part of the dining ritual. The person in charge of ablutions (body washing) carried a towel that the lord and his honored guests used for wiping their hands. To demonstrate that the water for ablution was not poisoned, the marshal kissed the wet towel on which the lord was to wipe his hands. By the sixteenth century, napkins, squares of cloth or paper used at the table for dabbing the mouth or hands while eating were an accepted part of dining. They were made in different sizes for different events (think of the lobster bib today).

Fashionable men in the late nineteenth century wore stiffly starched ruffled collars, which were protected with a napkin tied around his neck. The expression "to make ends meet" refers to this napkin.

Table Decoration

The difference between an ordinary table setting and one that sparkles is made by the table decoration. It can be a simple pair of brass candlesticks, which add charm, or an elaborate vase of roses, which adds romance and perfume to the aromas of the meal. Careful planning and attention to detail play a major part in creating a table setting with style.

In designing your table decorations, you should:

• Decide upon your theme, menu, and guest list. Once you have determined these issues, imagine your table setting. Envision how you want the table to look before the food appears.

• Be like the Victorians and use the appropriate dishes, flatware, and stemware. If you have inherited a set of dishes for 12 from your grandmother, use those pink flowered plates. Bring out the artichoke plates and the fish platter. You can always use dishes from another set for a different course.

• Find interesting table linens. Color is a foolproof scene-stealer. Maybe it is a standard tablecloth or an interesting bedspread!

• Select beverages or wines to enhance your menu and choose the appropriate stemware, including a water goblet.

• Choose your centerpiece carefully. Many choose fresh flowers or artificial, silk, cotton, or plastic flowers. Fruits, vegetables, and ceramic pieces also look attractive. You may have a wonderful collection of something that would be striking and fun as a centerpiece, to beguile the guests. Food can be decorative, too.

My mother often used a beveled mirror on a runner as a centerpiece, upon which she placed a lovely bowl of flowers. Sometimes she filled a silver epergne with flowers. I still use a mirror, but I like to use objects I have collected upon it: a rare mineral specimen, a jade statue, and an Ikebana arrangement. I use the centerpiece to express sentiments, celebrate time-honored occasions and seasons, or create my own statement.

In the following chapters, we see how many talented designers and decorators mix, experiment, and create their own table decor. Many added contemporary accoutrements to set off their inherited china and stemware. They found new colors to harmonize or draw out the colors from yesterday. They paired the antique with the new, the ornate with the simple. If they had it, they flaunted it. If they didn't have it, they punted. You can, too.

One hostess makes a graceful Ikebana arrangement.

Another uses a graceful dancer. *Courtesy of Siobhan Theriault*

An amazing candelabrum is a wonderful statement. *Courtesy of Mandarin Oriental Hotel du Rhône*

Food is always fun to play with.

There are so many possibilities.

Of course, you can place a collection of glass animals on a mirror and have a lovely centerpiece. *Courtesy of Siobhan Theriault*

Flowers and Table Decor

Celebrate occasions such as holidays, births, marriages, and life with floral arrangements. An easy, inexpensive decorating solution, flowers can enhance the ambiance of your table. Once candles and flowers were the norm. Today, people may place individual arrangements at each place setting, parade flowers down the table, or place a flower on each napkin.

If you do use a floral arrangement (which means you can call the local florist, visit the closest specialty shop, or head for the garden), keep them low or tall and slender so your guests can see and hear each other. Perhaps you want one dramatic bloom or maybe you want to give each guest an individual vase, or perhaps you want to march several arrangements down or around the table like a strand of pearls. Have fun with them.

Their holders are as important as they are. To avoid mishaps, be certain all containers are waterproof and sit on something that protects the table. Your vase should be firmly weighted so to prevent an arrangement from tipping. You may have a standard crystal vase or silver Revere bowl that you use on your table, or perhaps you prefer the whimsy of a basket or a cachepot. You can use a lovely cream pitcher or even inherited cigarette holders for small vases.

Whatever your style, flowers are the perfect way to add beauty and warmth, and create a space that reflects your personality.

A beautiful pink bouquet in a clear glass vase reflects the natural pinks of an evening sky. *Courtesy of Grass Roots Florist*

To fill a space, you might try a horizontal arrangement with lots of flowing greens. *Courtesy of Grass Roots Florist*

A formal setting, with deep red petals and several candles, makes a strong statement. *Courtesy of Lumiere Imaging*

A lovely bowl of tulips is reminiscent of Rembrandt's paintings. *Courtesy of Jennifer Drake Photography*

Roses have an immediate impact on a guest's happiness. *Courtesy of Grass Roots Florist*

2. Company's Coming

Many of us love to entertain; we enjoy good conversation, good food, and good friends. We like planning the menu, shopping for the event, and setting the table. Some of us even like smelling the air as the onions caramelize, marveling at the brilliant green of the kiwi as the skin slips off, or opening the mysterious pomegranate. Yes, entertaining can be fun!

But entertaining is about more than merely eating. It is about the whole experience, and table decor plays a significant role. The first perception your guests may have of the meal is the table and its setting.

Although general guidelines do exist for setting a table, tables should reflect our personal style and the mood we wish to create. Once setting the table meant adhering to the rules: today's table, however, can be contemporary or traditional, English country or retro. We can use all our lovely things that are normally tucked away or we can go to the local florist or supermarket. We don't have to be elaborate or expert. All the process really requires is the necessary tools and the basic knowhow. Once we have that, we can discard the rules and create our own.

Setting the Mood

We can add sparkle and elegance to the table with crystal or silver bowls, candlesticks, decanters, or beverage pitchers. For a colorful table, we can layer a striped charger with a complementary floral patterned dinner plate and solid colored salad plate. For a festive look, we might use different napkins as placemats at each setting. Whether the mood is relaxed and playful, or elegant and traditional, the most fashionable tables feature a charming interplay of designs and styles.

In setting the table, we can decide whether to use table linens or not. Many enjoy setting the table directly on the polished wood of the table. A tablecloth, table runner, or mats are also fine options. Sometimes, a solid colored cloth is covered with a smaller lace cloth. At another time, an all-lace tablecloth can be placed on the bare table to create a more elaborate look.

Courtesy of Mandarin Oriental Hotel du Rhône

Courtesy of Mandarin Oriental Hotel du Rhône

Table linens can help us create the ambience, which is so often touted in restaurant reviews. They come in many different colors, styles, and textures: from pure white to colorful printed cotton, from vintage, retro, damask to lace or linen. You can use your grandmother's lace cloth, a quilt, or even a shawl.

Cloth napkins are much more luxurious than paper. They can match the tablecloth or mats, but a contrasting color and texture can sometimes make a setting come to life. Dinner napkins are much larger than the smaller luncheon napkins. Napkins can be folded in many different ways. Just look under napkin folding on the Internet.

To give a table personality, we generally add a centerpiece, which, more often than not, is flowers. Many of us, however, have things that entertain us, intrigue us, or trigger those memories of places, times, and people. It is even nicer when we can share such items by using them as a dining table centerpiece rather than keeping them behind glass or hidden in the closet. They can serve as an icebreaker, as something to play with during a dull moment at dinner, or an object to marvel at.

For example, some of us have several of those attractive glass paperweights with flowery swirls inside sitting on a bookshelf somewhere. Those glass globes, encasing intricate designs of flowers, animals and swirling patterns, are attractive decorations. Many of the decorators featured have drawn on their collectibles or their inherited tableware to set tables that are supercharged with excitement.

A delicate porcelain figurine can become a lovely centerpiece.

Paperweights are usually seen on a side table or bookshelf, but they certainly can be used as a table decoration. *Courtesy of Siobhan Theriault*

Setting the Table

When the wealthy had servants, formal dinners used larger, more bulky knives and forks and more informal meals used luncheon size cutlery. In the 1950s, some companies made a third size, the place size, which is a compromise between the two.

Today, to set the table:

- Allow at least two feet for each place setting to eliminate that overcrowded feeling and place the settings at least 1 inch from the table's edge and squarely in front of each chair.
- Position your china and glassware in order of use. The soup bowl is placed on top of the dinner plate. The salad plate is located to the left of and just above the forks. The bread plate also is placed to the left and slightly above the salad plate.
- Place your silverware according to the order it will be used; first to be used is found on the farthest left and right sides of the plate. Place the knife to the right of the plate, with the blade facing the plate. Place your spoons to the right of the knife: first the teaspoon and then the soupspoon. Place all forks to the left of the plate, in order of use. The only exception is the cocktail/oyster fork (and when was the last time you saw one of those outside of a restaurant), which is placed to the right of the spoon.
- If the salad fork is to be used as a dessert fork, it is placed to the right of the dinner fork, next to the plate. The European style, which is quite acceptable, is to locate the dessert fork and spoon above the plate. The spoon, with its handle to the right, goes above the fork. Turn the fork's handle to the left.
- Glasses are generally arranged in a triangular formation with the water glasses closest to the plate. The wine glasses will go to the right of your water glass.
- Place napkins on the plate, to the left of the fork, or inside the glass. Napkin rings are an additional means of adorning the table.

Christina Gamota designed a placesetting for one who longs for an African safari. Notice her placement of the silverware and china.

Tuulikki's table has handpainted Valencia china and Costa glass. It also has Iittala vodka shot glasses and an 1867 sardine box. The swans were a wedding present.

The sixth egg was large and oddly shaped.

The baby duck grew into a beautiful swan.

Hydrangea Table

Color is key in table decor. Kate Dickerson Design set this table in an antique New England dining room, with original hand painted murals on the walls. The wall murals inspired the setting, which highlighted the lavender, rose, and green tones used throughout the room. Louis XV upholstered chairs provide comfortable seating.

The pink, lavender, and green grape on a butter yellow badckground tablecloth is by Pierre Frey from France. Lavender and rose French napkins are by Yves Delorme. Tiffany's "Chrysanthemum" pattern sterling flatware is set, in European style, with tines and bowls down, to show off the beautiful chrysanthemum pattern on the backs. The centerpiece is a potted hydrangea in a Chinese cachepot. Sterling candlesticks and silver and cobalt glass wine coasters are all family heirlooms. Alsatian green-stemmed white wine glasses and American pressed, green glass water goblets are set next to Limoges handpainted vegetable salad plates (depicting purple beets, rosy radishes, snow peas and artichokes), shown with Herend "Rothschild Bird" place plates. *Courtesy of Kate Dickerson Design, Inc.*

Wasabi Expertise

When they were young and possibly foolish, Mary Lou Touart's friend sent her a set of handmade pottery from Northern Japan. For years, she treasured it, using it to serve family and friends. She began to cook with soba noodles, sampled seaweed, and made tempura for her guests. She and her son even made a Parsons table to display it. Today, she has downsized and given the set to her daughter, who once again enjoys the china with her friends.

This setting is one of tremendous detail that brings together different regions and ages. The owner's grandmother bequeathed her the late nineteenth century silver spoons. Soup bowls are placed on two plates. The batik napkins are from Indonesia. The modern-day seed balls from China are placed on a large serving dish. The teacups have wooden saucers.

The owner and her son made the Parson's table. To achieve the deep red gloss, they covered it with 20 coats of Ford red car lacquer.

The King and the Ceramic Manufacturer

In the nineteenth century, the king of Sardinia required some replacement pieces for his set of Chinese porcelain. After a year of work, Herend, a Hungarian porcelain manufacturer, completed the replacement pieces and brought them to the king's castle. There, the firm's representative asked to be left alone to arrange the collection for inspection. After removing the original pieces and arranging them on a table , the firm's representative placed the Herend product into the cabinets. When the King and his courtiers entered the room, the representative presented the Chinese pieces on the table as his own work. After listening to the King and court complain that these items were not nearly so perfect as the porcelain in the display cabinets, the Herend representative revealed the truth.

The story spread, and the reputation of Herend's porcelain artistry became well known. The firm began to unveil new, original designs.

Gifted artists paint the Herend patterns. The techniques used today are the same as those of their forebears. *Courtesy of Martin's Herend Imports, Inc.*

Herend has consistently earned the respect of its peers throughout generations. *Courtesy of Martin's Herend Imports, Inc.*

The Collector and Chinese Exports

The owner, a collector and writer on American furniture, wandered into Chinese export porcelain when left a small collection of blue and white ware produced for the English trade in the 1770s. This inheritance led to further investigation and a collection of Chinese under-glaze blue and white export porcelain, with a focus on the work of the late Ming and early Qing dynasties.

The Chinese have long excelled in ceramics. By 618-906 AD, they had developed high temperature kilns and discovered the secret of porcelain. Then during the latter part of the Yuan Dynasty (1271-1368), potters developed lovely blue and white ceramics in which a very finely ground cobalt was employed for the color. This was painted on before the coating of glaze, hence the term under-glaze blue. Within a few years, the design was being outlined with thin, dark lines and then filled with different shades of blue wash. So successful was blue and white ware that 700 years later it's still being produced for export.

Blue and white porcelain was initially exported to Southeast Asian Persia and Turkey, but with the arrival of the Portuguese, it began to be seen in the West. Soon the Dutch entered the trade, first by the simple expedient of capturing Portuguese carracks on their way back to Europe. In 1604, the cargo of the ship *Santa Catarina* was auctioned in Amsterdam for an enormous profit, and within a few years the Dutch became active in the trade. In Dutch, carrack is spelled *kraak*, and this early export is now known as *kraak* porcelain; many of the surviving pieces are in Holland.

Although this late Ming Dynasty ware is distinctive, it is usually of indifferent quality. Dishes are thinly potted and casually decorated; the color is often a blue-gray. Typically, the glaze at the edges is chipped. Decoration is usually in the form of rectangular panels surrounding a circular central panel.

Far better quality is the export ware produced during the early years of the Qing Dynasty. With the exception of the early Ming dynasty, this is a high point in the production of blue and white porcelain. Here, we see smooth-surfaced, hard white porcelain with a clear even glaze and brilliant blue decoration.

Not until after the American Revolution were American ships able to trade directly with China. From the early years of the 1800s, a massive amount of blue and white Chinese export ware was made for the American market. The most common pattern is Canton ware, a standard pattern of blue and white porcelain, which was named after the Chinese port from which it was shipped. Canton ware is characterized by deep under-glaze blue color and a stock pattern featuring pine and willow trees, a pagoda, distant mountains, riverbanks, and a teahouse. The border almost always includes a distinctive pattern of semi-circles and diagonal lines, which are popularly known as "clouds and rain."

Center right:
This table is set with a good quality blue and white Chinese export octagonal salad or desert plate made for the European market, c. 1760. The flatware is by Tiffany.

Right:
This fine blue and white Chinese export porcelain dinner plate is from the K'ang Hsi era, 1662-1722.

A French Country Table

This decorator created an autumn table in russet and orange, using French Grange furniture. She elected to create a centerpiece, which marches boldly down the center of her long table. She reflected its colors in her elaborate folded napkins.

This design emphasizes the length of the French country table. The Swedish green glasses are used at the dinners for the Nobel Prize awards. The silk Crate and Barrel napkins are meticulously fanned. Each contains a fresh gold rose, which also rest on the French baguette baking paddle in the table center. The table has all the rich brightness of New England in the fall.

The pear plates came from TJ Max, the chargers are antiques, and the hand painted coffee cups are from a distant Finnish relative who painted for Arabia china.

The Special Occasion Table

Pink is the sweet side of red. It's sugar and spice, little girls, and cotton candy. The pink china many have inherited can seem insipid in today's world, but that isn't so when it is teamed with bright lime green. Now, it is a smartly sophisticated combination.

An innovative couple inherited the furnishings of his grandparents' home. Rather than selling them, they polished and shined and put them to use in their home. As we walked into the exquisite dining room, she said, "I don't do casual easily. I love to play with table decoration." She is gifted in her play.

Right:
When first married, the decorator bought the mahogany table and chairs second-hand. Later, her daughter asked her to store the Italian chandelier that she had discovered on a foreign trip. Rather than just store it, our clever decorator hung it, replacing her own crystal chandelier. She searched for complementary china and stemware to draw out the colors of inherited Haviland Limoges pink floral. Because the Limoges plates are smaller than customary plates, she sought a complementary size. The new under plate is Raynaud Limoges pink stripe. The deep pink crystal goblets were made in a Gibraltar glass factory. Their sparkling pink harmonizes with the Limoges pattern.

Below:
She inherited the etched goblets and the sterling silver, which she prefers to her own pattern. The knives have mother of pearl handles. The etched centerpiece and candlesticks were found in an antiques shop. She acquired the bright pink French napkins in Bermuda; the green placemats are hand-painted plastic. The setting is perfect with the room's decor.

Asian Dinner for Two

An Asian table setting calls for imagination. It combines layers of contrasting shapes, colors, and patterns through the cutlery, their rests, the plates, and the food itself. The meal is presented architecturally; everything is linear and angular around the softness and curves of the food, which has been chosen for its variety of colors and textures.

Small, delicate portions of food provide visual excitement. Traditional Japanese wisdom dictates a serving of eight colors during a meal, and thirty kinds of food during the day to ensure a well-balanced diet. *Courtesy of George Gamota*

Christina Gamota used her collections of Japanese dolls and lacquered boxes to create a striking setting.

The touches of red give an elegant look to this decor. *Courtesy of George Gamota*

Black by itself is striking! To get real drama and spark, pair black with white. The lacquered boxes and trays frame the food and dramatize the fare. On the sideboard, in front of a series of black and white etchings by Jacques Hnizdovsky, she sets out her dessert.

The Lost Necklace

Throughout the nineteenth century, the name "Rothschild" was associated with European wealth, luxury, and opulence. The Herend manufactory (of Herend, Hungary) immortalized the legacy of this amazing family by creating the "Rothschild Bird" dinnerware collection.

In 1850, the Rothschilds called upon the Herend manufactory to create a dinner service for their Vienna estate. Herend designed a dinnerware service that recounted a Rothschild family story in which Baroness Rothschild of Vienna lost her pearl necklace. The next day, a gardener spotted the necklace in a tree, where the birds were playing with it. The service was delivered to the Rothschild family in 1860.

This china creates a beautiful table. Many connoisseurs consider this porcelain china to be the paragon of hand painting on porcelain. Painted in twelve motifs, each represents the story of the lost necklace. *Courtesy of Martin's Herend Imports, Inc.*

A detailed border of green scales, perfectly complementing the greens of the pattern's foliage, accents the timeless elegance of this hearthside setting. *Courtesy of Martin's Herend Imports, Inc.*

Safari Dinner

Leopards, lions, jaguars, panthers, tigers, monkeys – they were going on a safari. She designed a table to evoke a distant locale.

The ferns and the design on the mats suggest a tropical rain forest. *Courtesy of Paul Doherty*

This fisherman belongs on a different continent. *Courtesy of Paul Doherty*

The magic and mystery of Africa are evident in this centerpiece. *Courtesy of Paul Doherty.*

Grandmother's Glory

Beginning in the early nineteenth century, China made Rose Medallion porcelain for export to America and Europe. It appealed to Victorian tastes because of its delicately detailed, fan-shaped medallions or little clusters of Chinese figures and flowers on a colorful background. A lovely legacy of the China trade, it is highly collectible and beautiful to own.

Half the pleasure in possessing heirloom china lies in the memories it conjures up. This particular setting recalls those pre-wedding festivities or a special birthday dinner.

Using heirloom china and glass, Tuulikki Loring and Anne Cuervo created this lovely setting for six in an Arts & Crafts room.

Antique lace mats rest on a pink linen tablecloth.

The pink and white rose centerpiece reflects the colors in the dishes.

The Rose Medallion dinnerware was exported in the China trade in the 19th century and belonged to Anne's great-grandmother. Two variations of the Rose Medallion pattern exist in the room: the classic style with four sections of roses, and a variation with two sections of roses alternating with two sections of people.

A Rose Medallion tea caddy and two girandole candelabra rest on the sideboard.

Hunt Season Dinner

Kate Dickerson Design set this table for a hunt season dinner in the mountains. Warm earth tones create a cozy setting. The table is draped with an antique Indian paisley shawl. Each autumn green linen napkin is gathered into a napkin ring of olive wood, which has been wrapped in a garland of quail feathers.

Austrian stag-handled sterling flatware and serving dishes are used with a variety of antique drinking glasses. Herend hunt plates, each hand painted with a different game animal, rest on Majolica pottery from Portugal. An antique German carved breadboard holds a loaf of rustic bread. *Courtesy of Jay Elliott Photography*

The centerpiece is a Majolica cachepot filled with various evergreens, oak leaves, corkscrew willow branches, pinecones, and pheasant feathers. Birch bark-wrapped candles flicker in glass hurricanes that are etched with hunting scenes. An antique bronze deer adds a regal note to the setting. *Courtesy of Jay Elliott Photography*

Study in Pinks

She is a beautiful, white-haired, twinkling blue-eyed potter. He is a charming silversmith, in the Paul Revere style. Together, they set beautiful tables and entertain many.

"When I was a little girl, " the owner told me, "This china was in barrels in the attic. My dad always said it belonged to my great aunt. Each flower is different."

When she was in college – long before she ever thought about marriage – she adored this set of lace mats, handmade in China, and bought them at a linen store that was going out of business.

Each flower is hand-painted.

The soup spoons, inherited from his family, are engraved with a seal that includes a clenched fist.

Some of the old tureens await use on the sideboard.

Some antique servers in contrast.

Her husband made the silver candelabra and the lovely ladle. He created the ladle in 1985 or thereabouts, from a round 5/8 inch diameter rod approximately five inches long, using the cold-forged process.

The World of Herend

Since 1826, Herend (pronounced HAIR-end) has produced some of the world's most distinctive and outstanding porcelains. The manufactory name is derived from its home in a small Hungarian village not far from Budapest. Ceramic production has existed for many generations in this region.

Created for Count Hadik of Hungary, in the early 1900s, this pattern is truly elegant. *Courtesy of Martin's Herend Imports, Inc.*

Herend's trademark basket-weave design and scalloped edges are set off with 24-karat gold bands. *Courtesy of Martin's Herend Imports, Inc.*

Harvest Table

In Christina Gamota's designs, there is a clear and formidable rhythm. This is craft as art.

Italian pottery plates portray a hunting scene, which is echoed by large rabbit figurines as the centerpiece.

On a flat-textured Ukrainian cloth, dried sunflowers on Japanese copper-colored leaves offer charm with cosmopolitan flair. The linen napkins resemble brown tree bark.

The goblets are Polish, and the water glasses are Mexican.

A Limoges Buffet

David Haviland, whose ancestors immigrated to America in 1640, set up a manufacturing establishment in Limoges, France, in 1839 to produce this china for export to the United States. Haviland china, translucent porcelain, is fired at a high heat, which seals the pattern in color so that it never wears off. In the late 1800s and early 1900s, the typical patterns were delicate pastel flowers with gilded touches.

Victorian ancestors would have been pleased to use these specialized plates.

Limoges fishplates are used in this Victorian buffet by Fancy Flea.

The centerpiece includes ornate gilded and crystal boxes and a remarkable fringed lamp.

Tudor Elegance

Gary Inman created a table setting in this Tudor dining room, with its hand-carved mahogany paneling, silver-leaf ceiling, Tibetan wool and silk rug, Italian silk drapes, silk string paper walls, and custom furniture.

White lilies, with bells of Ireland and red orchids, flank the chandelier, adding height and fragrance to the composition. *Courtesy of Thomas Kojcsich*

The long burgundy and gold silk runner adds a slash of rich Bordeaux style to the table, increasing the dramatic effect. It complements the gold chargers and red and gold floral plates. *Courtesy of Thomas Kojcsich*

Borsht Memories

The table is the heart of the home, in any culture. It is where families eat, drink, discuss, plan, philosophize, and celebrate. Christina Gamota's table represents treasures that her parents preserved and shared as well as new items that she bought on her visits to the Ukraine.

Black lacquered wooden plates with floral painting are from the Ukraine. Dinner is traditional with bread and borsht, served in Ikea's clear glass, square bowls resting on the floral plates.

The silver flatware is a family heirloom used on a hand-woven, Ukrainian coverlet that performs as the tablecloth.

A real sheaf of wheat enlivens the damask napkins.

The brass samovar and vintage canning jars beautifully coordinate above the sideboard with a dynamic oil painting that features similar items.

Fish and Guests

Good table decor is a way of marketing your meal. Even those who consider themselves amateur cooks can present an exciting table.

The antique soup tureen matches the under plates.

Generations of serving ware are mixed at this meal. The stoneware pitcher came from the Dearborn Museum store in Michigan, the fish sculpture is from the De Cordova Museum in Massachusetts, the chargers are antique, Makota Yabe made the soup bowls, and the hostess made the ceramic salad bowl.

3. Birthdays, Anniversaries, and Other Happy Occasions

Everywhere you turn, lives are filled with rituals. We have the smaller, more personal, significant ones and the grand, socially recognized ones like the annual holiday celebrations. Creative table decor can add to that festive feeling.

This Peanut Butter and Jelly Cake makes a colorful splash on any table. *Courtesy of Jennifer Zivolich Emery*

Happy Birthday

You say it's your birthday
It's my birthday too, yeah
They say it's your birthday
We're gonna have a good time
I'm glad it's your birthday
Happy birthday to you.
John Lennon and Paul McCartney, "Sixteen Candles"

How wonderful it is – no matter what age – to be honored by a birthday party!

Royal Doulton Birthday

Known as that " stoneware fellow from London," Sir Henry Doulton, who produced drainpipes and domestic stoneware, became a world-renowned ceramics giant. Over time, his firm became famous for fine bone china tableware and Staffordshire figurines, which have reflected the different tastes and fashions of the last 100 years. Although other manufacturers have imitated this style, Royal Doulton has incorporated its English heritage and cosmopolitan tastes with the past, present, and future.

Often, collections of these figurines stand on a shelf in a corner, collecting dust. This collector brought them out for a charming birthday party.

Courtesy of Paul Doherty

> *"There are three hundred and sixty-four days when you might get un-birthday presents... and only one for birthday presents, you know."*
> Lewis Carroll [Charles Lutwidge Dodgson], "Humpty Dumpty," *Through the Looking Glass.*

Courtesy of Paul Doherty

Birthday Tea

A froth of soft yellows and pinks establishes a spring-like ambiance for Elaine and Guy Doran's birthday tea party.

The lovely yellow and pink arrangement suits the small tilt-top tea table. For a sumptuous touch, cloth napkins each are decorated with yellow flowers and a fern, reflecting the yellow roses in the centerpiece. The hand-embroidered cloth sits catty-corner so the wood can be seen. The teapot is by Bing & Grøndahl, the teacups are English bone china, and the silver is by Christofle.

The Yellow Rose of Birthdays

Marked for Dessert makes spellbinding birthday cakes.

This elegant cake adorns a birthday dinner. *Courtesy of www.rickaguilar.com*

The cake has become the centerpiece, which certainly simplifies the table-setter's job! *Courtesy of www.rickaguilar.com*

Make a Wish

Marked for Dessert can craft a dramatic cake with intricate sugar flowers, ribbons, or bows. Their cakes certainly can take center stage!

A birthday cake, with a gold fondant flounce imitates the golden table linens from Sara James, Los Angeles—perfect for this birthday girl's glass of bubbly. *Courtesy of www.rickaguilar.com*

An elegant dinner party requires an elegant finish. This sleek chocolate bow cake with gold accents will complete the table setting and end the meal with flare. *Courtesy of www.rickaguilar.com*

> *On his eighty-fifth birthday (News Summaries, 20 August 1955), Bernard Baruch said, "To me, old age is always 15 years older than I am."*

You can choose an innovative architecture or presentation style for your cake, transforming it into any shape and structure that you can imagine. Choose a shoe-shaped cake for a dancer's birthday or fondant-covered lovebirds for a wedding shower. *Courtesy of www.rickaguilar.com*

Marriage and Beyond

Planning a wedding? One of the more significant events is the rehearsal dinner. Then there are the wedding festivities (see Chapter 6), anniversaries, and perhaps a baby shower.

Down on One Knee

Many of us want to propose marriage in a very special, memory-making way. Some are creative in this undertaking, while others struggle for the words or theme.

Rather than posing this momentous question on a billboard or at a public event, Tricia Traxler suggests an intimate dinner with your best friends.

Red enlivens passions, and this Chinese red dining room makes all occasions special – especially a surprise engagement celebration shared with close friends. Rich gold Anichini linens are set upon the gleaming Baker mahogany table. The champagne flutes represent love and prosperity for all. The table settings, which combine antique German silver with contemporary Christofle, are a composition of gold and silver.

Pheasant feathers in urns surround antique cherubs from Austria, while a bronze Cupid – wearing a gold heart necklace – gazes upon the scene. The *piece de resistance* is the spectacular old mine-cut diamond engagement ring set on a plate as a special surprise. Other place settings hold golden apples and pears. French angels anchor the ends, and moss-covered spheres are strewn about. A small German angel, hanging on a golden cord from the chandelier, floats over the scene to bless the event.

A Rehearsal Dinner

In the 1700s, porcelain was a prestigious status symbol, and Chinese porcelain coffee and tea services, with their delicately modeled details, cost vast sums. Many countries yearned to know how the Chinese manufactured porcelain.

After the first European porcelain was produced, in Dresden in 1709, many European kingdoms began making porcelain. In May 1775, the Royal Copenhagen Porcelain Manufactory was founded in Copenhagen, Denmark. The trademark is three wavy lines, which symbolize Denmark's three straits, the Øresund, Store Bælt, and Lille Bælt.

From the outset, the owners agreed that the greater proportion of porcelain produced would be painted blue before glazing. At that time, only cobalt blue could withstand the high temperature required to fuse the porcelain paste and the glaze. Since then, this beautiful indigo blue has become the factory's mark of distinction. Many collectors know the Danish Christmas plates.

Although the pattern originated in China and has been used by porcelain factories throughout the world, Royal Copenhagen's Danish Blue Fluted is considered the "true" Blue Fluted, because specially trained craftspeople in Denmark still paint the pattern by hand. Even today it takes 1,197 brush strokes to paint a Blue Fluted dinner plate.

This elegant table for a wedding rehearsal dinner celebrates life and is reminiscent of traditional Danish dinners. Elaine and Guy Doran used ivy garlands and gold ribbons to symbolize fidelity and marriage. A charming touch here is the decoration of each chair. The Dorans use Royal Copenhagen Christmas plates as an innovative wall covering for their antique dining room; others might use wallpaper.

Ivy wreaths, for the happy couple, even embellish the cupboard.

Elaine uses antique candlesticks around her arrangement of beautiful yellow raniculus and deep blue hyacinths, which harmonize with the blue in the china pattern.

The Anniversary Dinner

Christina Gamota designed a big occasion table in celebration of a twenty-fifth ("silver") anniversary.

The miracle of twenty-five years of marriage is celebrated with candlelight, silver, and roses. Candles march down the dazzling table where cupids, of course, hold the place cards. The glasses are Waterford's Lismore pattern.

A silver cow finial reclines on the antique butter dish.

The candelabra-lit sideboard holds an elegant covered serving platter.

The Victorian silver hearts for candy are astonishing and rare. The silver bird and rabbit figures are the work of the Italian luxury jewelry firm of Buccellati and part of their "Silver Menagerie."

Silver mint julep cups hold white roses with just a hint of blush. That hint brings out the richness of the mahogany table. The napkin rings resemble wedding bands; the silver flatware is by Gorham.

A Sixtieth Anniversary Party

A marriage 60 years old certainly needs to be celebrated—even if it is a simple celebration with old friends and family on someone's porch. Perhaps the easiest way—and perhaps the most beautiful—is to "say it with flowers."

The table has all the elements: flowers, candles, decorated butter, and wine. *Courtesy of Katherine Hilliar*

Roses are part of life.
Courtesy of Katherine Hilliar

Even the ham is decorated. *Courtesy of Katherine Hilliar*

A Hummel Baby Shower

Many collectibles tantalize with memories of people or remembered times and places. They captivate and enthrall us. Here, the hostess for a baby shower used her Hummel ceramic figurine collection, inherited from her parents, as the centerpiece for the party.

Talented German artist Sister Maria Innocentia Hummel developed a partnership with the Rodenthal, Germany, ceramic company W. Goebel Porzellanfabrik, to establish The Master Artists of Goebel, to transform her images of youthful children into a highly successful line of ceramic figurines. Sister Hummel died in 1946, at only 37 years of age, but to this day Goebel master artists discuss each new M. I. Hummel work of art with an Artistic Board at the Convent of Siessen.

Courtesy of Paul Doherty

Mother's Day Lunch

Tricia Traxler celebrates Mother's Day with a fairy-tale lunch which is quite appropriate, since many think of mothers as amazing creatures with supernatural powers. Moss, bird's nests, golden eggs, and birds—hand-carved in the Alps and enlivened by a fairy and a sprite—create a whimsical and beautiful luncheon setting.

Tricia found the hand-carved birds at the Salzburg Flower Market. They came from an elderly Austrian farmer who wiles away the winter by carving replicas of the local birds and making the walk down the mountain to the Flower Market in the spring to sell his wares. Each trip Tricia makes to Salzburg includes a stop at the market to add to the bird collection.

The Holidays

Holidays are wonderful times for decorating the house. While many books are devoted to the topic, we can suggest a few of the possibilities here.

Witches, Pumpkins, and a Night of Thrills

Halloween is a grand time for a party; everyone is in costume and ready for a big night.

Perfect decor for a Halloween party! *Courtesy of Design Ideas, Ltd.*

The rich and saturated colors of thick wool felt come close to capturing nature's autumn palette. Design Ideas reproduced shapes of familiar leaves in vibrant colors as placemats, trivets, coasters, and a runner that blends them together. *Courtesy of Design Ideas, Ltd.*

We Gather Together

Snow may be falling in northern climates, with wind wrapping the house in cold gusts of frost, but in the United States guests leave winter's chill behind at this Thanksgiving table. In front of a roaring fireplace, Elaine and Guy Doran set a hospitable harvest table of Swedish Rostrand china.

Flickering light from the fireplace indicates the season of short days and long nights. Canadian folk artist M. Arthur Bouchard carved the great turkey.

Over the fireplace, folk sculptures of birds and a running hare are enlivened with a garland of ivy.

'Tis the season to be jolly.

Deck the halls with boughs of holly. *Courtesy of Design Ideas, Ltd.*

Fa-la-la-la-la, la-la-la-la.

Fa-la-la, la-la-la-la-la-la.

Norwegian Supper Table

Christmas in Norway is long and filled with traditions and mythic characters, such as the elf-like *nisse*, who wears knee pants and a long red-stocking cap. Elaine and Guy Doran create a relaxing and sophisticated environment that transports a simple supper into the extraordinary. Bold colors in Scandinavian style emphasize the joy of the upcoming holiday.

An eighteenth century tavern table is set with Porsgrund porcelain in a charming Christmas pattern. The sugar container is an antique version of the china pattern. Fringed tulips in a pottery crock reflect the red in the china.

Provence-style Christmas Feast

A Christmas tradition in Provence, France, is to layer three tablecloths, to represent the Holy Trinity. Kate Dickerson Design used a cutwork cloth in white and an ivory linen from Waterford over an antique white damask tablecloth. The centerpiece is a melange of roses, evergreens, fruits, artichokes, and nuts. An apricot-colored wired organza ribbon, twisted through the arrangement, is used also to tie white damask napkins at each place. Kate chose the fruit, flowers, and ribbon colors to complement the dishes.

The plates are limited edition Daum from France, entitled "The Lost Arrows of William Tell." Each is hand-painted with a different fruit, including ribbons and arrows in 24-karat gold and platinum. They rest on Herend "Gold Border" plates, with arborvitae cuttings layered between for a holiday touch. Sterling flatware is Tiffany's "Chrysanthemum" pattern. Vintage water and wine glasses are different patterns of etched crystal. *Courtesy of www.jayelliottphoto.com*

The center arrangement is overflowing from a Herend "Rothschild Bird" tureen, with the lid placed on the table, next to it, as part of the arrangement. The lid handle is a hand-painted bird on oak leaves. *Courtesy of www.jayelliottphoto.com*

The arrangement includes coral- and apricot-colored roses mixed with artichokes; pears; red, green, and purple grapes; oranges; figs; and pomegranates. Evergreens include arborvitae and umbrella pine. Another Christmas tradition in Provence is having thirteen specific desserts, each with a meaning associated with the Christmas story. Nuts, figs, *callisons d'Aix* (almond-shaped cakes with white icing), dried grapes, nougat candy, pomegranates, pears, and other fruits are laid out in a colorful array on the alcove table. Antique silver fruit knives complement the old and new china, which includes Herend's "Queen Victoria" pattern. *Courtesy of www.jayelliottphoto.com*

Homemade liqueurs are served in a collection of Waterford cut crystal and antique etched crystal liqueur glasses. Demitasse cups and saucers are in Herend's "Rothschild Bird" pattern. *Courtesy of www.jayelliottphoto.com*

Christmas Breakfast

The *trompe l'oeil* painted kitchen walls and ceiling by Kate Dickerson resemble a traditional Provencal farmhouse. The copper chandelier is garlanded with laurel roping, red berries, and French wired ribbons. French country chairs have wheatsheaf backs. The tablecloth and napkins, in bright Provencal ocher colors, are by Yves Delorme, from France. The Majolica plates, from Portugal, mix well with antique pottery from Provence and pressed glass juice tumblers. The pearl-handled flatware also is French.

The meal includes croissants, French bread, a pot of freshly whipped butter, and individual ramekins of homemade apricot jam at each place setting. *Courtesy of www.jayelliottphoto.com*

The simple potted ivy topiary centerpiece has been "studded" with kumquats on hidden bamboo skewers, to resemble a miniature orange tree. *Courtesy of www.jayelliottphoto.com*

A plate rack holds a collection of French, Italian, and Portuguese pottery. *Courtesy of www.jayelliottphoto.com*

Frosty Frolic Land

Petite porcelain bisque figurines, or Snowbabies, appeared first in the early 1900s, but only in the late 1980s did a company that specializes in holiday collectibles, Department 56, begin to re-create them for the public. Every year, new Snowbabies are released, enabling enthusiasts to add to their collections.

Rather than keeping her collection behind glass, Elaine Doran brings them out during the holiday season.

This clever hostess set the New Year's table featuring various timepieces. *Courtesy of Whitney Gay*

New Year's Dinner

Should auld acquaintance be forgot
And never brought to mind?
...We'll tak a cup o'kindness yet,
For auld lang syne.
Robert Burns, 1796, from "Auld Lang Syne"

Crackers, beads, and red roses complete her design. *Courtesy of Whitney Gay*

4. Affairs Of The Heart

Her eyes twinkling, she told me this story:

The morning was rain-washed. The sun shone in prisms. I wore my new pink dress. I was alone – very alone – and so was he. We both had been alone for what seemed like an eternity.

On the way to the concert, we talked about this and that. When we reached our destination, the sun was shining brightly. The new summer warmth electrified everyone.

We walked with our friends to the agreed-upon picnic spot under the tall pines. I had brought my special cookies – hermits – and crisp white June peaches. He had brought a wine redolent of spring breezes and strawberries. Our friends had brought a triple crème and Stilton cheeses, water crackers, a whole-wheat boule, and hazelnuts. We dined in the shade under the tall pines.

By the time the conductor had begun to play, he was sitting next to me. His hand reached for mine.

That summer we moved to the rhythms of planting and weeding. The sun and the rain. The sky was cloudless and intensely blue, the gardens ablaze with orange tithonia and golden sunflowers, we were awash with a new light.

Today, we still look for romantic moments.

Wine, cheese, and a lovely Tiffany swan. What else could you want?

Tell Me When

Many adults enjoy together a pre-dinner drink, or as the French say, an *aperitif*. It may be a simple glass of dry white wine, Champagne, or Dubonnet. Wine, champagne, or cognac: each carries a flavor of romance.

Shaken or Stirred?

Olives or with a twist? Dry or extra dry? Straight-up or on the rocks?

The gin Martini always has had a certain mystique. Some people recall actor Humphrey Bogart's classic line in the movie *Casablanca*, "Of all the gin joints in all the towns in all the world, she walks into mine."

Gin was considered urbane, sophisticated, and just slightly naughty. In the 1930's movie *The Thin Man*, actor William Powell instructed his bartender, "The important thing is the rhythm. Always have rhythm in your shaking. Now a Manhattan you always shake to fox-trot time, a Bronx to two-step time, a dry Martini you always shake to waltz time."

Commuting husbands drank Martinis in the club car of the train. Women wore aprons and chilled Martini glasses at home. Butlers and short-skirted waitresses passed trays of Martinis, in the black and white movies.

Some of us may remember the "Martini Scene" in Casablanca.

There, with a martini ready to go, Humphrey Bogart, says "Here's looking at you, kid."

The Night They Invented Champagne

Louis XV's favorite, the Marquise de Pompadour, who knew many of the greatest artists and philosophers in the mid-1850s, proclaimed, "Champagne is the only wine that leaves a woman beautiful after drinking." Napoleon's mother and his beautiful wife, Josephine, adored champagne. Napoleon said, "I drink champagne when I win, to celebrate... and I drink champagne when I lose—to console myself." Actress Sarah Bernhardt drank a half-bottle of champagne with her meals, confessing that the bubbles had a marvelous effect on her.

Champagne is a drink shared with our loved ones, as Tuulikki Loring demonstrates here in a private garden. Associated with joy and festivity, its meaning and appeal are universal. Although popular, champagne coupe or saucer-shaped glasses were not intended for drinking champagne. (Legend says Marie-Antoinette's bosom was used to model the shape.) Instead, long-stemmed flutes or tulip-shaped glasses are designed to enhance the flow of bubbles and concentrate the aroma of the wine.

Many ships have been launched with an exploding bottle of champagne. Many marriages have begun with a champagne toast. Many New Years have been welcomed with the pop of a champagne cork (although the bubbles are wasted when the cork is popped). As the saying goes, "The ear's gain is the palate's loss." Instead, the cork should come off with a quiet sigh.

Good Wine

According to Iago, in Shakespeare's *Othello*, "Good wine is a good familiar creature, if it be well used." Aperitifs, or drinks consumed before the meal, became popular in the late nineteenth century, in Europe. By 1900, Americans were whetting their appetites with aperitifs, too.

This Herend porcelain dragon dish guards a bottle of wine and offers food to spark the appetite.

Majolica ware, the most celebrated Italian pottery, has bright, fresh colors. Mary Lou Touart set up a wine bar using an antique Majolica spittoon to hold sheaves of grain. An oyster plate awaits its duty.

Do you remember your lemonade stand? This one is just a little more sophisticated.

Caviar Valentine

A valentine means not only that especially selected greeting card sent to a special person on Saint Valentine's Day (February 14th), it also is a token of love or a person singled out as one's sweetheart.

Today, a highly regarded token of love is a sensual Valentine's Day dinner. Now, if you don't want to cook, you, like Christina Gamota, can create a pretty, modern-day Valentine's dinner of champagne, caviar, and fresh strawberries.

Angels and statuary in this unique setting make an amusing decor.

When Life Gives You Lemons

On those hot summer days, that nice, tall, cold glass of lemonade can slide down so easily.

On the vintage tablecloth are Elsa Peretti's hand-blown thumbprint, Venetian crystal plates and bowls. Tiffany flutes, black lacquered bracelet napkin rings, and Peretti's sterling bone design and clear crystal candlesticks accompany them.

Valentine's Day with Bubbles

Love feeling sensual? Want to breathe romance?

You probably have other places in your home that offer opportunities for loving tenderness and fanciful libations. Tricia Traxler celebrates Valentine's Day with billows of fragrant bubbles, a cup of coffee (you could use a *coup de champagne*), and smiling cherubs graced with jewels.

Imagine the look on your sweetheart's face if you unplug the phone, lock the door, light aroma-therapy candles, and turn on the water. Bubble baths aren't just for kids, and this tub fits two. Her angels and statuary bring the outside in.

Sugar and Spice

Some may think of France when they hear the waitress rattle off, "We have strawberry crepes, chocolate mousse, *tarte tatin*, and *creme brulee*, " while castanets clatter in their heads when they hear, "flan." The salvia begins to run, and stomachs begin to growl. Desserts are the forbidden fruit today, but can you imagine life without them?

Coming to America

In the early 1920s, a young man decided to leave Denmark to find his fortune in the United States. Just before he emigrated, he met blue-eyed Ulla, and they were betrothed. Ultimately, she convinced her large and loving family that she should join him in the United States, and his family gave her the money for the ship's passage. She arrived in Boston on February 22, 1926, but her ship remained outside the harbor because customs officials did not work on George Washington's birthday. Once she finally arrived and until she married her Swend, she lived in Lexington, Massachusetts, with a family who paid her room and board ($7 a week) as compensation for her household work.

When the young couple ultimately visited Denmark, in 1934, for a belated honeymoon, they were given this coffee set, which they packed in a steamer trunk to be taken back home to the states. But when they returned, they found that many pieces of the set had not survived the journey. Over the years, their family members replaced them, piece by piece. Seventy-six years later, Ulla still sets a Danish coffee table.

The silver coffee set is embossed with delicate, old lace patterns. Contemporary white, square platters bearing chocolates and strawberries counterbalance the dainty sterling and porcelain Victorian demitasse cups and saucers.

The silver is from Georg Jensen. Ulla had the Oddfellow spoon made by a relative for her husband.

A traditional Danish coffee table service in the Blue Fluted pattern includes matching candlesticks. The hand-embroidered tablecloth was made to match the china.

Dixie Heirloom

The story goes that the original owner of this large set of mid-nineteenth-century dishes packed them in barrels before the Siege of Vicksburg, Mississippi, during the War between the States. Eventually, the set came to light again. Half came North with one descendant while the other half remained in the original Southern kitchen. The descendants like to believe that the mistress of the plantation served Yankee generals sumptuous meals on this china, while surreptitiously collecting money for the Confederate cause. Stories like these make dessert and coffee with this set especially fun.

This china has many different pieces, including hot chocolate cups and compotes. *Courtesy of Siobhan Theriault*

Courtesy of Siobhan Theriault

"You're the Cream in My Coffee"

Since the Boston Tea Party in 1775, Americans have been enjoying a caffeine surge with tea or coffee. When prohibition was mandated in 1920 banning alcoholic drinks, sales of coffee skyrocketed. Today, even middle-schoolers drink frothy caramel and coffee concoctions.

Legend has it that a shepherd noticed his sheep dancing and prancing after eating the red "berries," or beans, from a shiny green coffee plant. Upon eating several himself, he became as hyperactive as his sheep! His fellow villagers found that the berries helped them to stay awake for their prayers.

Ottoman Turks introduced coffee to Constantinople around 1453.

Feeling threatened when coffee was first introduced to Italy, wine merchants there appealed to the Pope to ban it. Instead, the Pope liked the aroma so much that he tasted the brew and pronounced coffee a Christian beverage. *Courtesy of Tuulikki Loring*

Tea and Spode

During the nineteenth century, the dining rooms and parlors of wealthy people were social centers of the home. The dining room was filled with stylish furnishings, flowing linens, elaborate tableware, and a large assortment of dishes and glassware. Formal dinner parties there consisted of tremendous amounts of food; of course, you were not expected to eat everything.

This melon-form silver teaset was made in Edinburgh in 1825. Notice the rose finial.

This table is set for a buffet dessert party. The peach-colored, c. 1817 Spode dessert service has plates in many shapes. The Sheffield silver candelabras were made around 1812.

Cordials and Espresso

Tuulikki Loring likes to serve cordials and espresso at the end of a meal. She sets up an elegant sideboard using her heirlooms.

The sideboard is ready with Royal Crown Derby cups and a silver coffee pot.

Coffee in the Living Room

Many hostesses like to move the dinner party from the dining table after the main course and serve dessert in the living room, where guests can be more comfortable, stretch their legs, and can continue to enjoy the party. The table can be cleared at a later time. Christina Gamota places desserts on a salver here.

Christina Gamota creates a simple yet elegant setting with Waterford's Lismore brandy glasses, a decanter, and a small sterling plate. She has found a new use for an old ashtray; it holds the ginger.

After-dinner Cognac

During the seventeenth century, winemakers from the Cognac region of France initiated the process of double distillation, allowing a concentrated alcohol, or *eau-de-vie*, to travel safely. Stored in oak barrels, the wine was meant to be diluted upon arrival at its destination. Over time, however, they realized that the *eau-de-vie* improved with time and its contact with the oak wood, and was quite enjoyable without dilution. Soon, the wine was called "Cognac."

The Cognac region in France was then primarily Protestant. When French King Louis XIV cancelled the Edit of Nantes, which had guaranteed freedom of faith, worship, and a safe haven for all, many Protestant families left France for England, Ireland, or Holland. Some began to import the *eaux-de-vie* produced by their Cognac relatives and, by the nineteenth century, trading houses shipped their Cognac products abroad in bottles.

5. Breakfast, Lunch, and Tea

Breakfast and lunch entertaining can be a time to have some fun. You can catch up with friends and reflect on the week just past, plan the week ahead, or celebrate a special occasion, such as an engagement or graduation. Certainly, these days, one ought to celebrate when and where possible. More than ever, people want easy, do-able, and fun ways to make everyday life meaningful. Of course, the best place to make this happen is at home.

Salad for two. *Courtesy of Design Ideas, Ltd.*

Breakfast for one can be special. A simple splash of red — strawberries, cherries, or jam — gives a plate a festive appearance. *Courtesy of Miranda Burnett*

Elegance & Simplicity Wedding & Event Designers produced this lovely buffet arrangement for a special day. *Courtesy of Thomas Van Veen Photography*

Breakfast

During the week, breakfast is often a hurried affair. But during the weekend, breakfast can be a time of luxury and enjoyment by indulging in a few extravagances: a robust coffee, eggs Benedict, French toast, or *crème brulee*. By using special salt and pepper shakers, heirloom cream and sugar servers, and the morning paper, you leave no reason for your loved ones to rush out the door.

Breakfast in Bed

"It's all in the details," as Karen DeKoker's design points out. A bowl of cereal is one thing, but that same bowl, on a doily, on a tray, with a vase of flowers, handsomely folded napkin, and fine silverware is certainly another.

Imagine the aura of joy you create, as your special someone awakens to see their favorite breakfast in front of them. You don't have to cook it, if you don't want to. Many places offer lovely take out menus. The surprise is the thing. *Courtesy of Siobhan Theriault*

Let the light in slowly. Set down the tray. *Courtesy of Siobhan Theriault*

Breakfast for Two

Table setting, according to Christina Gamota, is a matter of balancing different items and accessorizing properly. Peggy Wright, a gifted artist, made the large blue ceramic bowls, which sit on round white Rosenthal plates. The handles on the glass and stainless Alessi cups bring out the blue of the pottery.

Breakfast with Guests

A weekend brunch can be a slow and wonderful world apart. You can indulge in robust coffee or maybe a lovely strata, perhaps some interesting sausage, and bagels, of course.

The glasses are crystal; the flowers are fresh. *Courtesy of Siobhan Theriault*

This table, created by Karen DeKoker, reflects the greens in the stained glass window. *Courtesy of Siobhan Theriault*

Breakfast at the B&B

One hundred and thirty miles of barrier islands compose the Outer Banks landscape of North Carolina: unmatched beauty and rich natural resources. Miles of national parks and wildlife refuges greet visitors—whether they were the original English settlers or modern tourists today.

> *John Gunther proclaimed, "All happiness depends on a leisurely breakfast."* (Newsweek, *14 April, 1959*)

Like many places in the area, The Duck Inn incorporates this picturesque view of the sound.

This seashore B&B serves lovely breakfasts, day after day. Salty mists quicken the pulse as the room resonates with nautical decor.

Lunch

The name given to a meal between breakfast and tea (or dinner) is lunch. When dinner is the main meal, or held at an early hour, lunch was a light collation. In the earliest meanings, lunch, or luncheon, meant a thick piece of bread, bacon, meat, and maybe some cheese.

My grandmother used to entertain her sewing circle members over lunch. They would sit at the large mahogany table, clad with lace mats, and dine on creamy chicken Tetrazzini, deep fried chicken croquettes with almonds, or a sherry-laced chicken-a-la-king. Those were the days when people didn't worry about calories, cholesterol, or food allergies, and everyone ate what was served. They were also the days when people like my grandmother paid someone to do the cleaning up!

Today, many people go out for lunch, but eating at a friend's kitchen table or on their porch can be much more rewarding: no restaurant noises, no interruptions ("Hi, my name is Bryan and I'm your waiter"), no fussing about the bill. If you don't want to cook, you can always "take out" at your local fancy food shop.

Italian Soup Luncheon

Soup is a comfort food, whether it is served from a crock pot or an exquisite Meissen tureen. Kate Dickerson Design, Inc. set the table for a meal of hearty Italian soup, on a short printed tablecloth of blues and yellows draped over a floor-length cloth woven with the same colors. The French wheat-sheaf chairs have rush seats.

The printed tablecloth sets the stage for a pattern-on-pattern tabletop, with handpainted plates (each one different) from San Gimignano of Italy. The Majolica wheat-sheaf pitcher and pearl-handled flatware are from France. Hand blown glasses are from Biot in Provence. *Courtesy of Kate Dickerson Design, Inc.*

Notice changes in the colors according to the light. *Courtesy of Kate Dickerson Design, Inc.*

Spring Luncheon

Whether you welcome a new baby, a neighbor, or hold a parents' and teachers' club luncheon, the mid-day meal can be festive. Christina Gamota uses sharp spring-green bowls to invoke springtime.

The white and green table decor reflects the springtime green outside. The grasshopper ornament also brings nature to the table.

Even the soup has a slight green hue.

Asparagus Celebration

In the nineteenth century, the *nouveau riche* enjoyed complicated table settings. They had oyster plates, artichoke plates, asparagus plates, and more. The first-of-the-season native asparagus is always an occasion for celebration, and for using an antique platter decorated with *bas-relief* asparagus.

Like oysters, asparagus is a luxurious seasonal food deserving of its own dish. The tableware is imported from China. The frozen pansy ice ring keeps wine chilled and the advent of spring in mind.

A simple dessert is made elegant in a compote or wine glass.

Sing a Song of Soup

Whether it is potage, bouillon, broth, gumbo, bisque, consommé, or chowder, soup is a nourishing meal that also can be a pretty occasion.

Against the winter snow, Tuulikki Loring sets out a lunch for two on white lacy mats. The chairs are unique art themselves. *Courtesy of George Gamota*

Purple bowls glow against the snowy scene.
Courtesy of George Gamota

> *Miss Otis regrets she's unable to lunch today.*
> Cole Porter, "Miss Otis Regrets."

Tea (or Coffee) for Two (or Four)

According to Chinese mythology, in 2737 BC, while the emperor was sitting beneath a tree, his servant boiled drinking water. A leaf from the wild tea tree dropped into the water. From that leaf developed the custom of drinking tea. As Buddhist priests moved around China and Japan over the following centuries, the cultivation and drinking of tea followed them.

By the Tang Dynasty (618 AD to 906 AD), tea became China's national drink. In the sixteenth century, Portuguese merchants opened sea routes to China, and The Dutch East India Company began to import tea to Europe in the early seventeenth century. Tea's subsequent popularity worldwide played an important role in opening Asia to outside commerce.

During the latter part of the nineteenth century, afternoon tea was a major component of civilized British life. It is said that Anna, Duchess of Bedfordshire, began sipping tea and eating a few cakes in order to satisfy her hunger between lunch and dinner. Finding that the refreshment satisfied her, she told her friends about how to prevent hunger pangs.

Word of her advice spread far, and today more people drink tea than any other beverage except water.

> *"There are few hours in life more agreeable than those dedicated to the ceremony known as afternoon tea."*
> Henry James

My Cup Runneth Over

Even a solitary person can set a pretty table, sit down, sip tea, and enjoy peaceful and good feelings about the world.

Mary Lou Touart fixes a cup of tea to enjoy on her porch.

The Tea Party

Among lovely American antiques, Christel McCarthy hosts a sherry and tea party for four, with assorted pink lusterware dishes, c. 1830. A bowl of fresh fruit complements.

The tablecloth is pink linen, the English teapot is by Mason's, and old sherry glasses blend with the stopper of the Baccarat decanter.

Just One Lump Please

The clink of fine dishes, the aroma of Earl Grey or lemon ginger tea, the sinful indulgence of fine pastries... afternoon tea is synonymous with sophistication and elegance.

Fancy Flea Antiques developed a tea party around a combination of dishes that all include different pink flowers in their decoration, including a Chinese charger in the background. The silver tea set includes a candy basket and grape scissors.

This is an unusual Limoges asparagus dish and silver asparagus server.

Afternoon Coffee

Reminiscent of a scene right out of a Paris bistro or the Italian countryside, the afternoon light infuses this afternoon coffee setting with golden hues.

Tricia Traxler collects Venetian masques and uses one to adorn her Baker coffee table done in the Biedermeier style.

> *"Tea, to the English, is really a picnic indoors."*
> Alice Walker, *The Color Purple*

The centerpieces contain red calla lilies, red sand, and floating candles. Red rose petals are spread on the tables. *Courtesy of celine@piecemontee.com*

Perhaps this magical ball will transform someone's life. Courtesy of *celine@piecemontee.com*

Say It with Roses

Taking inspiration from nature, this Grass Roots installation displays traditional qualities with the strong lines of the chairs, the place settings, and the roses. The addition of a line of graceful candelabra, with rounded candleholders through the center of the design, creates a sense of unity in the midst of contrasts.

The repeated patterns in the placement of the materials in this design are a delight. *Courtesy of Grass Roots Florist*

The high-branched, ivy-twined candelabras lend a delicate grace to the linear line of chairs and place setting materials. Their curved stand mimics the curve of the lily pads behind them. *Courtesy of Grass Roots Florist*

As the evening goes on, the candles are lit, lending yet another spot of brilliance to the design. *Courtesy of Grass Roots Florist*

Snow White Wedding

In the traditional Brothers Grimm version, Snow White is born to a queen, who dies shortly after giving birth. The king takes a beautiful but proud new wife. She possesses a magic mirror, to whom she would often ask "Mirror, mirror on the wall, who's the fairest of them all"? Much to her delight, the mirror would always reply, "You are." Then one day, much to her horror, the mirror replied "Queen, you're the fairest where you are, but Snow White is more beautiful by far."

Every woman wants to be the most beautiful of all on her wedding day. Piece Montee created a Snow White theme for a winter wedding on a romantic cruise in Paris on the river Seine.

Snow White would have approved of this lovely design. It sparkles with frost. Candles float in blue lichen surroundings. *Courtesy of celine@piecemontee.com*

The floral arrangement is perfect for the Snow White theme. *Courtesy of celine@piecemontee.com.*

The table twinkles in the reflected light from the glasses. *Courtesy of celine@piecemontee.com.*

Here, the materials are not seen as petals per se but as beautiful objects with distinct shape, color, and texture. *Courtesy of Grass Roots Florist*

A Bed of Roses

Grass Roots Florist uses rose petals as a red carpet ceremonial.

This design is fluid – and expressive — as a child's finger painting. *Courtesy of Grass Roots Florist*

Royal Purple Wedding

Cleopatra, the famous Egyptian queen, loved purple. To obtain one ounce of Tyrian purple dye, she had her servants soak 20,000 Purpura snails for 10 days. Purple is a royal color. Piece Montee created a purple and white theme for this wedding.

This table makes a striking visual image with its square purple arrangement of white orchids, purple moss, and purple callas in a square glass vase. *Courtesy of celine@piecemontee.com*

A white and purple frame designates the table. The fabric of the wedding dress and a white butterfly are ornaments. It is inscribed "jour de bonheur" (day of happiness). *Courtesy of celine@piecemontee.com*

Embroidered purple ribbon napkin rings carry out the color scheme. *Courtesy of celine@piecemontee.com*

The guest favors are personalized shiny pyramids containing sugared almonds. *Courtesy of celine@piecemontee.com*

The bridal table is the picture of elegance. *Courtesy of celine@piecemontee.com*

New England Fall Wedding

Autumn's crisp chill and vibrant color provide the perfect backdrop for a wedding in New England. This wedding table decor melds both history and cosmopolitan flair.

Two glowing roses and an apple – what could be more perfect? *Courtesy of Capture Photography*

A simple mason jar can make an excellent bouquet holder during your reception or the perfect vase for a fall outdoor wedding. *Courtesy of Capture Photography*

Long beige napkins, a rustic lantern, and simple rose and apple candles create a simple but elegant look for this fall wedding. *Courtesy of Capture Photography*

Simple menu cards at each place setting can tie monograms and wedding colors into your wedding table decor. *Courtesy of Capture Photography*

Rose Red

Queen Marie-Antoinette said, "And I will make thee beds of roses, and a thousand fragrant posies." If love could be defined by one symbol, it would be the rose. Throughout the centuries, the rose has played a significant part in romance. No other symbol can evoke the same feelings of romantic love. Perhaps that is why the rose is everyone's (slight exaggeration, here) favorite flower. Grass Roots Florist created this beautiful scene.

Red roses always make a statement. *Courtesy of www.baronspafford.com*

Especially when there are so many of them! *Courtesy of Grass Roots Florist*

This is a wedding that people will talk about for months to come. *Courtesy of Grass Roots Florist*

Even the beverage table is color coordinated! *Courtesy of Grass Roots Florist*

Fairytale Wedding

Once upon a time, a spoiled, selfish young prince lived in a shining castle. One winter's night, an old beggar woman came to the castle and offered him a single rose in return for shelter from the bitter cold. Repulsed by her appearance, the prince turned the old woman away, but she warned him that appearances could be deceiving, for beauty is found within. As punishment, she transformed him into a hideous beast and placed a powerful spell on the castle. The spell could only be broken if he could learn to love another and earn her love in return.

In a beautiful medieval French castle near Paris, Piece Montee created a Beauty and the Beast atmosphere through artful table decor.

The room is an elegant room complete with oil paintings of ancestors and elaborate woodwork. *Courtesy of celine@piecemontee.com*

Piece Montee covered candelabras with feathers, suede, flowers, golden threads, sparkling pearls, dried fruits, and even sweets. The tables are decorated with gold and red petals.*Courtesy of celine@piecemontee.com*

The red apple – from the Snow White legend perhaps — is transformed into a candle, for a red passion ambient. *Courtesy of celine@piecemontee.com*

Consider the Lilies of the Field

Lily blooms are the highlight of the garden. Long lasting as cut flowers, they generally bloom between June and August. The large, trumpet shaped flowers feature a variety of colors and designs.

Lilies can have breath-taking color. *Courtesy of Grass Roots Florist*

Often, however, they are used in their pure white form, marking the significance of the occasion. *Courtesy of Grass Roots Florist*

Those Long Feasting Tables

According to the dictionary, a banquet is a sumptuous entertainment of eating and drinking. Sometimes, it can be even thought of as a feast, followed by dancing or speeches. Grass Roots Florist uses repetitive arrangements to give the long banquet tables a special cadence.

The banquet table holds spring floral arrangements. *Courtesy of Grass Roots Florist*

Transforming this simple hall into a spring fantasy. *Courtesy of Grass Roots Florist*

Spring Wedding in Montmartre

In the mid-1800s, many artists came to live in Montmartre, an area in Paris. By the end of the century, Montmartre and its Left Bank counterpart, Montparnasse, became the principal artistic centers of Paris.

Such artists as Pablo Picasso, Camille Pissarro, Amedeo Modigliani, Vincent van Gogh, Henri Matisse, Pierre-Auguste Renoir, Edgar Degas, Maurice Utrillo, and Toulouse-Lautrec worked in Montmartre.

This artistic area was the inspiration for Piece Montee's design for a spring wedding. The yellow, gold, and blue floral arrangement rested on a woody base. Yellow rose petals were spread all over the tables, and yellow candles or roses floated in glassware for each guest.

Each guest has a yellow floating rose in glassware. *Courtesy of celine@piecemontee.com*

Each guest also receives a yellow floating candle. *Courtesy of celine@piecemontee.com*

This traditional French restaurant was the scene for this wedding. *Courtesy of celine@piecemontee.com*

Spring means delicate flowers and soft green buds gently unfolding to cover the bare trees. Hopefully, it means love is in the air, and the world coming alive again after the dreary winter. *Courtesy of celine@piecemontee.com*.

The yellow, gold, and blue floral arrangement on its woody base and the floating candles create the atmosphere of spring. *Courtesy of celine@piecemontee.com*

Wedding Cake Decor

Of course, most brides require some sort of wedding cake. Like everything else, the couple's selection of a style for the wedding cake is influenced by fashion, cultural backgrounds, and traditions.

Today, another lovely dessert may precede the cake. Most weddings, however, feature a dramatic cake with elaborate icing, which may coordinate with the wedding colors. These cakes are decorated with intricate sugar flowers, ribbons, or bows, hand-modeled sugar figurines, real flowers, and/or cake topper decorations. Inside is the couple's favorite combination of cakes, fillings, and frostings.

The traditional circle is still a popular shape, but hearts, squares, ovals, and hexagons are also in demand. Some couples are choosing their tiers to be made in assorted shapes such as a square, a round, or an oval tier. A popular choice is the edible stack of hatboxes, cupcakes, or gift-wrapped presents tied with bows that cascade down the sides of the tiers. Of course, each tier can feature a different flavor too.

Since the wedding cake is a beautiful (and expensive) part of your wedding, it should be displayed prominently. Ideally, it should have its own table where it can be admired by all of the guests. Some use cake stands; others may use arches, flowers, or balloons.

The decor for the wedding cake table can be simple. Usually, there is a tablecloth, which may be the basic white or the wedding theme color. Tulle with or without white Christmas lights, greenery, and/or flowers can dress up the table edges. To add sparkle, rose petals, loose flowers, or silver or gold confetti can then be scattered on the tabletop.

Others have a theme cake such as a seashell or starfish at a destination beach wedding. If you have a certain theme, you can incorporate it into the cake table. For example, if you have a beach theme, scatter shells around the table and decorate the area around the cake with small shells. For an autumn wedding, scatter bright red crabapples and purple grapes around the table.

You can decorate the table further with your cake knife and server and your toasting glasses. Some brides decorate the table with framed copies of their wedding invitation or their engagement photos.

Mark Seaman of Marked for Dessert designed this stunning, five-tiered masterpiece studded with hand-rolled fondant pearls at the intersection of criss-crossed embossing on iridescent fond. A simple fondant drape and small cascade of sugar roses complement the bridal bouquet. The cake is displayed on a simple silver cake plateau with a beading design that reflects the same beading used in the cake's design. *Courtesy of www.rickaguilar.com*

Designs by Dorian created an extravagant flamingo-topped cake for a beach wedding. *Courtesy of www.DesignsbyDorian.com*

Two whimsical pink flamingos stand on a pink and white rose garden with calla lily accents. The groom sports a top hat and bow tie, the bride a veil and eyelashes; her toenails can be painted for an extra touch of whimsy. The base is a choice of pink or white with iridescent rainbow glitter dust to complete the design. *Courtesy of www.DesignsbyDorian.com*

This wedding cake, made by Marked for Dessert, is adorned with lilies made entirely from sugar. A fully dressed cake certainly decorates a table. The mirror creates an overwhelming display. *Courtesy of www.rickaguilar.com*

This cake by Designs by Dorian features a crystal model of the Eiffel Tower (Paris, France) surrounded with blue roses and forget-me-nots, white roses, and cascading calla lilies on a grassy garden. The lighted design shown is elegant yet simple, pure white. Lighting is disguised beneath the tower and in flowers. *Courtesy of www.DesignsbyDorian.com*

For this cake, created by Designs by Dorian, a white Southwest Native American wedding vase, finished in a horsehair glaze, rests upon a sandstone-textured base with a dream catcher, dove feathers, and roses. The wedding vase has been a part of Pueblo life for centuries. The spouts represent two separate lives while the bridge at the top joins these lives as one. The dream catcher captures the couple's bad dreams, doubts, and fears while allowing only the good dreams to pass through. Finally, the two dove feathers at the back of the design symbolize love—one for the bride and one for the groom. The feathers used in the floral design are also dove feathers. *Courtesy of www.DesignsbyDorian.com*

7. Wedding Table Decor

Judy Lewis, HudsonValleyWeddings.com

What do flowers, feathers, frames, fans, and frothy white tulle have in common? They are just a few of the many items that become tabletop decorations at weddings. Albeit the traditional floral centerpiece takes first place for wedding table decor, many brides look toward the unusual, the extravagant, and sometimes the downright strange to decorate their tables in a unique and memorable way.

The table decor creates the first impression that guests have at a wedding reception. The choices that the bride and groom make reflect their style and welcome their guests in an aesthetically pleasing way. Whether the decor is simple or extravagant, if done in good taste and forethought, the table decor can become the "wedding snapshot" that remains in the minds of guests long after the wedding is over and the tables are cleared.

Traditionally, wedding colors that are most frequently used are white, silver, and gold. Today's brides have taken to using almost every color, including black, to create a mood — from romantic and glamorous to Medieval and Gothic, to fun and funky, and everything in between.

Retail stores and on-line wedding shops offer a seemingly endless list of table decoration options and as many table favors. The decorations seem to fall into several categories, with the line between one and another sometimes blurred. What follows are several categories and some of the decorations that are available.

Ethnic or Cultural

Many of today's couples are honoring their ethnic and cultural heritages by choosing table decor that reflects their backgrounds. For some, the selection is both obvious and abundant, such as with a Japanese, Chinese, or Asian wedding theme. Just a few of the Japanese table decorations that are available, for example, are paper lanterns, fans, chopsticks, sake cups, and lucky cats, which can be integrated into the theme.

For Italian couples, a traditional wedding decoration is confetti flowers and Italian ribbon flowers. These flowers hold Italian Jordan almonds, which symbolize the wishes for health, happiness, fertility, prosperity, and long life. More extravagant versions such as calla and rose almond holder bouquets and bouquets that hold five Italian almonds wrapped in tulle are also available.

Balloons

Balloons are synonymous with celebrations. The simple balloon bouquet has been expanded to include balloon sculpture and intricate and elaborate centerpieces. Whether the decor is inexpensive or elaborate, using helium-filled balloons with sandbag weights always symbolizes festivity.

Balloons also make it really easy to decorate in keeping with a theme. For example, should the bride and groom pick a Cinderella theme wedding, there are Cinderella castle white latex balloons and bunches of related Cinderella-related items such as plastic castle containers, 3D castle centerpieces, castle metallic centerpiece kits, Cinderella castle card boxes, Cinderella coach confetti cards, Cinderella coach wedding favor hinged boxes, and much more. The same holds true for almost any theme that the couple can conjure up.

Candles, Candleholders, Candelabra, and Wedding Lights

Light and joyous occasions are a great match, because they create an atmosphere combined with gentle illumination. It's no wonder that candles, candleholders, candelabra and wedding lights are available in great numbers and styles. Brides can choose from a large selection of specialty lights as well as traditional favorites such as mini and net lights: Golden Canopy Lights, Commercial Mini 50lite String, Clear Lamps, Mini Lights, Frost Lamps, Twiggies (Rice Lights), Lighted Bells Shape, and arrangements such as bowls of floating candles, alone or combined with tiny flowers. The variety of candleholders is also immense, ranging from traditional candlesticks to elaborate candleholders.

Decorative Feathers

Feathers, real and synthetic, are available in a myriad of colors and sizes. A feather placed in each guest's empty wine glass, feathers tied around napkins, feathers dusted around each table's centerpiece and even, in theme, a feather in each wedding invitation can be a light and cheerful way to decorate. The theme can be completed with a shower of feathers released from overhead netting, during the first dance of the evening reception.

Confetti

Confetti is a part of celebrations such as parades and bon voyages. It's no wonder that it has found its way into becoming a wedding decor classic.

The extensive range of table confetti allows the couple to mix and match to stay in the color theme and to create combinations that say "fun." Confetti, for example, is available in unique versions such as large hearts that pop up and become 3D. Confetti can make its first appearance in the couple's invitations and be carried through to the tables. For couples who are concerned about the environment, table confetti can be water-soluble and biodegradable.

Flowers and Flower-Based Decorations

For the traditional bride and groom, flowers are the only table decoration they need or want. The evolution of the floral centerpiece results, in large measure, from floral decorators who do more than put a bunch of flowers into a vase. Their creativity becomes evident in the choice of flowers, containers, design, and arrangement. A professional florist can meet almost every budget, and the truly budget conscious can put together one or more flowers as a centerpiece, which will add color and, sometimes, fragrance to the room.

For those who love floral table decor, but don't want to deal with the issues that live flowers carry with them such as wilting and staining, there are a number of choices. There are silk rose topiaries in pots, silk roses in terra cotta pots, and many other varieties of other silk flower centerpieces. These permanent centerpieces provide lasting beauty and become part of the couple's home decor as well as a wonderful reminder of a very special day.

Theme Decorations

Many brides and grooms are designing their weddings around a theme that has special meaning to them. The couple that met at a beachside resort may choose a "beaches" wedding theme, which is developed with table decor. The beach theme may include miniature white Adirondack chair cardholder, soap or candy shells in mesh bags, candle holders with resin shell base, shell jewelry boxes, coconut candles in sea grass basket, or ocean bubbles.

If your theme is water, how about some sailboats holding your candles? *Courtesy of Design Ideas, Ltd.*

These sailboat pics could carry out your sailing image even further. *Courtesy of Design Ideas, Ltd.*

For a special wedding, for example, a florist can obtain black, deep purple, or very dark red roses, which can be part of a centerpiece. Unusual lovebirds, such as black ravens or crows with burgundy eyes, sitting on black tree branches on a "landscape" provided by deep burgundy and black roses and a sprinkling of iridescent black glitter, complete the mood design.

For couples who want their table decor to sparkle, decorative glitter adds that element when sprinkled randomly on the table, around the centerpieces or place settings.

Edible Table Decorations

Cotton candy, an ever-popular county fair and circus treat, has found its way into table decor in sweet centerpieces. Guests enjoy this centerpiece in more than one way, during or after the wedding reception.

When it comes to edible decor, hand-crafted marzipan designs are interesting, elegant alternatives. Designers use marzipan paste, which is individually hand shaped, molded, or sculpted into different "objects," among them fruits and flowers.

For the couple who wishes to entertain their guests with table decor, wedding table talkers are a unique choice. The concept is simple: each guest chooses a question from a tin, for example, and shares the answer with tablemates, a process that is meant to be an icebreaker. Content is inspirational in nature and provides opportunity for wedding guests to connect during the reception meal.

Several companies make "floral" centerpiece creations from a variety of candies, in simple bouquets or elaborate designs. Guests can enjoy them after the reception is over.

Party Crackers

Traditional party favors in England, paper poppers or "crackers," have gained widespread popularity at holiday celebrations throughout the world. As a logical extension, they can appear as wedding favors and have made their "debut" in the arena of wedding centerpiece decor. Available in thousands of unique color effects, they may contain a popper, a paper party hat, and/or a joke or riddle. Several companies even produce them from chocolate.

As the wedding table decoration is the focus of a guest's attention, it can express a couple's own style and creativity. Whether the mood of the party is formal and elegant or informal and playful, a smorgasbord of table decorations is available.

8. Candlelight After Dark

According to Mother Goose,
Jack be nimble
Jack be quick
Jack jump over the candlestick.

Today, candlelight fills us with thoughts of romance, but in days of old it was an absolute necessity. Europeans developed candles in the eleventh century. By the Renaissance, wealthy homes and churches were using them.

In colonial America, illumination by candlelight was necessary, expensive, and labor intensive. The fortunate wife boiled down the ox and mutton fat, following the slaughter of livestock by the men. She would skim it repeatedly to eliminate all the impurities. Ultimately, she would have a large kettle of pure tallow to make her candles.

During the fourteenth century, the Persians introduced the socket candleholder/stick to the Europeans. By the seventeenth century, its use had surpassed that of the pricket, which held the candle on an iron spike.

Since most candles shed dim light, they needed to be in close proximity to the user. Consequently, candleholders were portable. Think of the pictures in your version of *Mother Goose*. The chamber stick, a short candlestick on a saucer-like base with a handle, was designed for carrying from room to room, particularly to the bedroom.

Most early immigrants to America packed one or more candlesticks. Specialists know that early brass candlesticks were imported because zinc, a basic component of brass, was not discovered in this country until 1837. Iron and tin, however, were accessible at an earlier date, and candlesticks made from those materials could be inexpensively made in America.

Light the candles. Pour the wine into your glass. *Courtesy of Mike & Sonja Photography for Grass Roots Florist*

Candles come in many different forms and varieties. *Courtesy of Design Ideas, Ltd.*

Their shimmering light makes everyone beautiful. *Courtesy of Design Ideas, Ltd.*

Candle, roses, and hearts make a lovely Valentine's centerpiece. Seen a different way, the same centerpiece could cheer up someone recuperating from surgery. *Courtesy of Siobhan Theriault*

Candlesticks often contain a collar to catch dripping wax. Over time, drip pans moved up the stick until they surrounded the socket and became smaller. Consisting of a socket and collar at the top of a candlestick, a bobeche is a refinement of the drip pan used to catch drips. It is detachable for ease of cleaning.

Unlike electric light, candles always add charm and elegance. Light them just as your guests are seated for dinner. Candles should be either above or below eye level. Ten-inch candles are suitable with tall holders. Put extra long ones in lower holders. Groups of large round and square candles create interesting and colorful focal points for a table when they are comfortably below eye level.

This container could be a pond for your living room, a planter box for your dining room, or a candle stand for floating candles. *Courtesy of Design Ideas, Ltd.*

Candles in the daylight are as generous in scale and attitude as these Santa Barbara dining room pieces. *Courtesy of Stanley Furniture Company, Inc.*

These Lanta tea lights, carved from a single branch of a sustainably harvested mango tree, are at a traditional height. *Courtesy of Design Ideas, Ltd.*

These elevated tea lights in these innovative tall holders are designed to cast light down rather than up. Consequently, they chase shadows away from instead of into the corners. *Courtesy of Design Ideas, Ltd.*

If you have a dimmer, lower the intensity of the electric light. If your choice is lights on or off, turn them off and add sufficient candles so everyone can see.

Your collection of candleholders and candles should be varied and include decorative as well as plain ones. With an interesting mix of styles and materials, you can readily change your table's style.

Stack these candleholders like children's blocks to make a fascinating centerpiece. *Courtesy of Design Ideas, Ltd.*

This floral candelabrum makes a strong statement. *Courtesy of Grass Roots Florist*

You will believe that light can float. These vases use a hidden clear-cut glass cup to hold a candle in thin air. *Courtesy of Design Ideas, Ltd.*

A forged metal tree can be as simply elegant or as lavishly ornamented as you like. You can decorate it with candles or dress it in garlands, ornaments, and flowers. *Courtesy of Design Ideas, Ltd.*

Candles can be a major decorative element on a table. When mixed with flowers, they add magic to the scene.

A pretty candle and some flower petals make a lovely centerpiece. *Courtesy of Grass Roots Florist*

You can easily make this simple arrangement or re-create it, using a different theme. What about a Valentine's candle with candy hearts or rose petals? Or a candy cane pillar candle and peppermint candies for a holiday wedding? How about a pumpkin candle with fall leaves? *Courtesy of Grass Roots Florist*

A group of low, medium, and tall candles can help to set that special mood. To avoid a discordant look when you cluster candles, put them in holders made from similar materials.

The inner, color-changing LED light show in these ivory candles makes a dazzling centerpiece. *Courtesy of Design Ideas, Ltd.*

This candle and holder resemble the tight cluster of a plant bud. As a centerpiece, they convey the simple serenity and comforting promise of renewal. *Courtesy of Design Ideas, Ltd.*

A collection of brass candlesticks makes an elegant display. *Courtesy of Siobhan Theriault*

Candles give a lovely light, making people look especially beautiful in the flicker of their flames. The glow warms our spirits and illuminates understanding in our hearts.

Dramatic table settings result when candles are used, alone or in combination with other items.

Certainly, candles and flowers are often combined for a fashionable and often inexpensive wedding centerpiece as in this Grass Roots Florist design. *Courtesy of Luminere Imaging*

Candles and a collection of silver baby cups placed on a mirror make a dramatic centerpiece. *Courtesy of Siobhan Theriault*

In the mid-nineteenth century, silver napkin rings were used to identify a person's heavy damask napkins that could be reused for several meals before being washed. They became a traditional gift to mark the birth of a baby (engraved with the infant's name or initials and the birth date), to celebrate a wedding or anniversary, or at Christmastime. *Courtesy of Siobhan Theriault*

9. Decorating With Food

Decorating with food can be good for the body and the soul. Fruits and vegetables can enhance floral arrangements and give unique style. Mixing them with fresh flowers can add a certain amount of *je ne sais quoi* to your table. A vase of lemons, for example, hints at all the wonderful food to come while incorporating herbs and greenery conveys tabletop aroma and color.

Courtesy of Siobhan Theriault

Courtesy of Grass Roots Florist

Courtesy of Grass Roots Florist

Courtesy of Grass Roots Florist

Garden Wedding

Stelle Events designed a garden wedding dinner served family style. The fruit centerpieces gave the guests something visually tantalizing to entice them to the next course.

Guests' escort cards are decorated with botanical images of the fruit, which appear at their table. Each table has matching menu cards. At the Orange Table, for example, a beautiful menu card, which alluded to the amazing dinner to come, welcomes guests to the table. *Courtesy of Angela Lang*

At the Fig Table, the figs and olives mingle – as did the guests, who munched on olives between courses. Eventually, the family style entrée platter is placed on top of the olive saucer – just a bit of height so that everyone can reach with ease. *Courtesy of Angela Lang*

At the Grape Table, luscious grapes surround the family style platter — also tempting guests to savor the centerpiece in many ways! Satin ribbon entwined with the grapes and olive leaves adds a touch of elegance. *Courtesy of Angela Lang*

Many different kinds of melons adorn the Melon Table. Some melons are sliced open so guests can marvel at the translucent interiors. Salt and pepper are displayed in mini terra cotta saucers. *Courtesy of Angela Lang*

Instead of a large wedding cake, guests choose their own individual wedding cake. Reflecting the garden atmosphere, these cakes are exhibited on large terra cotta saucers raised on overturned terra cotta pots, which rest on decorative herbs. *Courtesy of Angela Lang*

Italian Evening Wedding

Italian food is greatly loved and tirelessly imitated the world over. It has been a source of endless pleasure and *joie de vivre* for many. In another wedding designed by Stelle Events, the table decor incorporated the abundant fresh produce found in Italy.

Centerpieces combine local flowers and berries to create rustic autumnal arrangements. *Courtesy of Meg Smith*

A long table adds to the rustic and intimate Italian dinner. Blankets on the chairs are added for guests' comfort and, if necessary, warmth. *Courtesy of Meg Smith*

Incorporating the abundant fresh produce found in Italy, elegant Bartlett and D'Anjou pears are nestled in a bay leaf garland decorating the table. *Courtesy of Meg Smith*

Colorful daisies wrapped with ribbon decorate the bride and groom's chairs. *Courtesy of Meg Smith*

Ocean Front Wedding

The first gift that her fiancé ever gave her was a blue topaz necklace because it matched her eyes. The happy couple and Katering by Kim used that color as their theme in designing the destination wedding buffet.

The wedding was small, but everything was garnished with abandon, letting the guests know that it was a beautiful affair.

Food was artfully arranged and garnished. The theme was the bride's blue eyes.

Cheese and fruit were plentiful and dramatic.

The cake continued the blue theme.

Courtesy of Grass Roots Florist

Think of your food as an art form that you arrange or sculpt, if you wish, for your table. The reason that some of these items below look so appetizing is that the presentation seduces us into believing an artist is at work.

Their pastries make you dream of dinner. *Courtesy of Knut Wefald*

As for their cakes…wow! *Courtesy of Knut Wefald*

And the glace fruits….maybe that's why Paris has so many tourists! *Courtesy of Knut Wefald*

Playing with Food

"Don't play with your food" is a common statement that many of us have heard, but food can be playful.

One creative hostess used Joost Elffers' book *Play With Your Food* (Stewart, Tabori & Chang, 1997) to carve imaginative, often beautiful, creatures from everyday fruits and vegetables. In fact, she had her New Year's Eve guests hunting for faces and body parts through her collection of fruits, vegetables, cloves, and peppercorns.

Vegetable art goes back to the sixteenth century. Certainly, we often designate people as different types of fruits or vegetables, e.g., "He is round as an apple. She is shaped like a pear."

The process begins with picking a fruit or vegetable that suggests a new image. This potato only needed legs and eyes.

Under the green stems lie interesting creatures; this started as a pear.

A new image accentuates the food's appeal.

Inventing new creatures raises food to a higher level.

Children of all ages can enjoy the playfulness.

Decorating with Food Guidelines

• Any garnish should complement the dish. To insure compatibility, use one of the ingredients in the dish, but in a different form. For a fish dish in which lemons have been used, ring the fish with lemon slices. If your dish is a complicated dish, use a simple garnish, e.g., chocolate curls on a chocolate mousse cake.

• When deciding on garnishes, think creatively. Stay out of the olive or paprika rut, for example. Colors should harmonize. The flavor of a garnish should complement the food.

• Arrange your meat and a contrasting vegetable on the same platter, which is much more attractive than having the meat on one platter and the vegetable on another.

• Whether you're serving the food on platters or plates, present the food (or garnishes) in geometrically pleasing shapes. For instance, make carrot curls, half lemon wedges, or cucumber fans. If you don't want to get out your knife to make diamonds or flowers, chopped parsley can do wonders. Alternate the heights of the food items. For example, lean a chicken breast against a mound of rice instead of just laying the two side by side.

• If you are plating the food, don't overload it.

• Odd numbers of food items on a plate are more pleasing to the eye.

• Place food on the plate just before serving it. A warm salad is not fun. If the food is cold, the food and the plate should be cold. If the food is hot, the plate should also be hot.

• Except for birthday candles and/or statues on a cake, do not decorate your food with anything inedible. Better to be safe than sorry! If you are using flowers, use organic edible flowers.

10. Around The Garden

Although the history of the United States is one of clearing land and building villages and cities, citizens have always admired the "purple mountain majesties." Our barbecues, porch suppers, and terrace dinners provide opportunities to enjoy the beauty of land in the cool evening. A combination of plants, garden art, and garden structures can provide further enjoyment for guests.

Today, the outdoors often has been integrated into the home. Family rooms extend into porches and garden rooms. These areas give a special, intimate place where we can relax and reflect, sheltered from the cares of the world. An oasis inside the home, these whimsical, playful places provide a place for peacefulness.

Dinner in the Garden

In the late afternoon or evening, after the activities of a long and busy day, we take our rest. Children might play flashlight tag or catch fireflies in a jar, within friendly confines of the neighborhood, while adults rock in their chairs telling stories, watching the stars, even singing some songs. The neighbors might drop by as the lights of the night slowly turn on.

Courtesy of Grass Roots Florist

Courtesy of Grass Roots Florist

Courtesy of Baron Spafford

Courtesy of Knut Wefald

Summer at the Seaside

Kate Dickerson's passion for rich colors is evident in this summer design. Here, she decorates this table in orange for the sun and turquoise for the water. As she says, these complementary colors are "the ultimate colors of summer." When used together, they make each other really pop.

Modern lacquered plates and bowls are set next to hand blown glasses from Biot, France, and antique English ivory-handled silverware. She took fresh garden-picked nasturtiums and nestled them in a blue glass. Her table arrangement stands silent among the flowers in the garden, signaling the beauties yet to come as the visitor walks through the garden. *Courtesy of Jay Elliott Photography*

The tablecloth is a nubby woven (washable) silk throw in aqua blue, draped with a runner of "Cotignac" fabric from Designer's Guild. Orange napkins are tied with polka dot ribbons for a touch of whimsy.*Courtesy of Jay Elliott Photography*

Hosta At Your Porch

When the summer sky is flat and almost white with heat and everything living is stilled by the sullen humidity, dinner on the porch (with fans stirring the breeze) can be a welcome respite. Tuulikki Loring and Anne Cuervo set a charming dinner on the porch. They took some deep red linens and china in the same colors and put them against the dark green foliage – and voila!

The lovely setting leads the eye from the table to the beautiful view.

The napkins are a variation of the red of the tablecloth, just as the Spode Indian Tree pattern has many colors within it.

Terrace Dinner Alfresco

Africa draws many of us with its huge plains, rivers, and night sky that stretches from horizon to horizon. Christina Gamota designed an audacious table setting, which is African in feeling. The textures are metal, wood, glass, and stone.

On black round straw mats from Neiman Marcus, she places Danish stainless steel chargers and white stoneware dinner plates. Black soup bowls punctuate the linear motif. Chunky sorbet glasses are from Crate and Barrel; the crystal tumblers are from Ralph Lauren.

Supper On The Porch

Ira Gershwin wrote, "Summertime, and the livin' is easy/ Fish are jumpin' and the cotton is high." Summertime is special – even the air is different; it smells sweeter, infused with the scents of the ocean and steak on the grill.

Memories of childhood and gracious living in a fine Southern novel come to mind when we see Tuulikki Loring's impressionistic table in soft pinks and greens on this shaded porch.

This table decor flows into green leaves on the other side of the porch screen.

The shaggy whiteness of this floral arrangement accentuates the pinkness of the setting. *Courtesy of Tuulikki Loring*

The Majolica earthenware plates are distinctive. Babylonians originally produced such sculpted and glazed ware in the ancient Middle East.

Dinner for Two

Design Ideas make tables interesting and fun with their sophisticated finishes, fluid shapes, and ease of use.

Courtesy of Design Ideas, Ltd.

Poolside Supper

Tuulikki Loring enjoys the world of nature. Here, she sets up a summer supper for four on a lace covering placed on top of a linen cloth. Her guests will dine with the flitting butterflies in this emerald oasis.

Burn citronella candles around the party area and have bug spray available for guests to use.

Use crystal and china to design an intimate setting. One of the best parts of owning a pool is sharing it with others on a hot summer evening.

Sushi in the Guest House

Who said you should always eat in your dining room? If you look differently at your home, you probably can find many rooms that could be used for relaxation, pleasure, and entertaining.

Tricia Traxler takes her guests outdoors, to the guesthouse on a hill surrounded by charming gardens. Part of nature, yet sheltered from the elements, this room provides a respite from a more formal entertaining. Lighting is candlelight from sconces around the room as well as a wire chandelier over the table. This magical candle-lit place becomes a get-away for dreaming, musing, and fanciful feasting. She serves sushi for four on ceramic garden seats at a round table covered with a velvet cloth. Decorations are beautiful shells collected around the world.

The chopsticks are Christofle polished ivory resin and silver etched.

The room is painted in garden colors of soft violets and greens, with an evening sky painted on the ceiling. The linens are green.

"I See the Moon...

...and the moon sees me." As day turns to night, a special time or magic hour emerges. The light of the day fades into the blackness of the evening, with new shapes and shadows. Tuulikki Loring designs a moonlit dinner for a small terrace.

The night is filled with mystery. *Courtesy of Tuulikki Loring*

The darkness adds immediate glamour. The rising moon creates pools of radiance. *Courtesy of Tuulikki Loring*

A moonlit dinner is always desirable. *Courtesy of Tuulikki Loring*

Breakfast in the Garden

Breakfast outside can have a clean severe purity. No longer do you have the hum and beep of the household appliances, the ring of the phone, the chatter of the TV – instead you have different aromas, sounds, and smells.

When morning has broken, Tuulikki brings coffee outside. Her breakfast decor is her garden.

Courtesy of Tuulikki Loring

"I've Got the Sun in the Morning"

(Rogers and Hammerstein)

A beautiful morning can bring forth songs of joy. Many people are avid collectors of Noritake white, translucent porcelain from Japan. Since the early 1900s, wholesalers have imported it to America. Initially, the delightful patterns were hand painted; today, they are transferred to the plates.

Tuulikki Loring found this pretty handpainted Noritake breakfast set for two at a church fair. It was a wedding gift to the original owners.

Tuulikki sets out a romantic breakfast for two.

Party in the Garden

Arranged flowers in your garden may seem like an odd concept. But they, like garden ornaments, can frame views, create vistas, and provide perspective. They point the way so your visitor can see the gorgeous stand of Asiatic lilies without noticing the fading alliums. Ideally, your garden arrangement can stand silent among the flowers, signaling the beauties yet to come as the visitor walks through your garden. Instead of you hustling your visitor around the garden, saying, "see this and that," a vase defines the view without you acting as the talking guidebook — defeating the whole purpose of relaxing in the garden.

Feast your eyes on a lovely jewel-toned bouquet. *Courtesy of Grass Roots Florist*

Some garden arrangements provide destinations; others call us to explore further. They can provide balance and texture, fill empty spots, and add color to heighten interest. *Courtesy of Grass Roots Florist*

Vivid arrangements in a garden setting accentuate verdant expanses surrounding them. *Courtesy of Grass Roots Florist*

The combination of formally contained flowers and flowers in their natural environment is one of the secrets of the perennial pull of garden decor. *Courtesy of Grass Roots Florist*

11. Show Me The Money

Increasingly, not-for-profit organizations are sponsoring benefit tea parties, fine wine and art, dinner auctions, cocktail parties, and late night suppers to generate income. Table decor can play a large role in these events.

Elegant events can be great fun.
Courtesy of George Gamota

Red Hot and Georgian

The music of American Jazz greats Ella Fitzgerald and Louis Armstrong inspired Gary Inman's tablescape, which features Steuben's Georgian vase. Planned as a late-night supper, the table skirt is corseted to create a sexy tone. The diners are provided champagne, strawberries, and decadent red chocolate tortes.

An explosion of red roses with pink and green accents from tulips, ginger, and orchids takes center stage. *Courtesy of Thomas Kojcsich*

Red votives, black sequins, and "red hot" candies complete the table. *Courtesy of Thomas Kojcsich*

The trumpet, microphone, and gloves on the chair are a reference to the intended diners, Louis Armstrong and Ella Fitzgerald. *Courtesy of Thomas Kojcsich*

Arabian Nights

Rhodec International created an Indian Enchantment table design as part of the 'Dining by Design' benefit for The Design Industries Foundation Fighting AIDS (DIFFA)sponsored by *Elle Decor* magazine and Taittinger champagne. Participants were invited to create an imaginative 11 square-foot space, which included a table with seating for 10 people and a vessel for chilling champagne. The tables were put on public display in New York City and auctioned off to groups of diners for the "Bubble Blast" gala.

This Scherazade setting emphasizes rich, jeweled color and texture. Over-sized palms entice the diner. Luxurious embellished saris form an overhead canopy, while screens of beaded fretwork and a painted silk panel provide the exotic backdrop to this opulent venue. *(Photos courtesy of Fiona Worboys*

Theatrical overtures define this lavish table setting.

Napkins folded to resemble peacocks, complete with tail feathers, highlight the fun nature of this event.

The central arrangement features luscious blooms and jeweled champagne corks.

A gleaming copper champagne vessel is held aloft by a platform of three elephant sculptures and intertwined with a floral garland.

A hand painted metallic goddess provides a dramatic background for the table.

English Tea

Gary Inman designed an English tea decor for an event sponsored by William Yeoward, the well-known English designer.

Courtesy of Thomas Kojcsich

Note the mirrored top and the use of crystal in the design. *Courtesy of Thomas Kojcsich*

Afternoon Tea is Served

The Victorians enjoyed their tea parties and staving off pre-supper hunger pains with thin sandwiches, small biscuits or cakes, and a special fruit or Madeira cake. Today, home tea parties and fundraising tea parties are becoming so common that stores are offering an increasing number of tea accessories, including several varieties of decorated sugar cubes!

The Lexington Field and Garden Club and Historical Society teamed up to raise funds to benefit a new kitchen facility at the historic Buckman tavern on the Lexington Battle Green.

The tables exhibited the members' talents and collections. *Courtesy of Mary Nokes*

The fundraising event was held in the to-be-renovated Depot building. *Courtesy of Mary Nokes*

> *"I shall sit here, serving tea to friends. . ."*
> T.S. Eliot. "Portrait of a Lady."

Teddy Bear Tea

If you go down to the woods today
You're sure of a big surprise.
If you go down to the woods today
You'd better go in disguise.
For ev'ry bear that ever there was
Will gather there for certain, because
Today's the day the teddy bears have their picnic.

As part of its fundraising effort, the Lexington (Massachusetts) Historical Society and the Field and Garden Club, jointly held a teddy bear picnic. Each table was differently decorated.

Do you remember those words? We all love teddy bears and what a wonderful theme for a fundraiser. Bears are popular animals, and probably the most beloved is Winnie the Pooh.

According to the storytellers, during World War I, Canadian troops on their way to Europe stopped at White River, Ontario, where Lt. Harry Colebourn bought a small female black bear cub for $20 from a hunter who had killed its mother. He named her 'Winnipeg' (after his hometown of Winnipeg) or 'Winnie' for short.

Those days were certainly different from now. Not only did Winnie become the Brigade's mascot, she also went to Britain with Lt. Colebourn and his fellow soldiers. When the brigade was sent to France, Colebourn loaned Winnie to the London Zoo. Ultimately, Winnie became a part of the zoo. There, A.A. Milne's son, Christopher Robin, played with her – inside her cage! The Lieutenant's bear was Christopher Robin's inspiration for calling his own teddy bear Winnie or Winnie the Pooh.

And that was the beginning of A.A. Milne's book *Winnie the Pooh*, published in 1926. It and successive books became very popular and have been translated into almost every known language.

A Teddy Bear tea is a popular way to raise funds. Many enterprising volunteers, again from the Lexington Field and Garden Club and Historical Society, designed this fundraiser.

"The way you wear your hat /The way you sip your tea.
Ira Gershwin, *"They Can't Take That Away from Me"*

Resources

Photographer **Hilary Argentieri**'s images aim to secure not the subject of the piece, but the genuine essence of the moment. Her art has been showcased in the national magazine *Peterson's PHOTOgraphic*, featured in the *Boston Globe* newspaper, and exhibited in the international volumes *The Best of Photography Annual* each of the past four years. The lead photographer for Capture Photography, she is currently engaged in bringing a fine art approach to wedding documentaries.
Rochester, New York
info@capture.bz
www.CaptureEverything.com

Karen deKoker's interest in creating beautiful table settings began in early childhood when her mother and grandmother would turn an ordinary mealtime into a fun and interesting celebration. Her homes have ranged from traditional to contemporary to historic. This experience has provided her with the opportunity to express her love of interior design, decorative painting, flower arranging, and gourmet cooking and to design an eclectic, warm, comfortable environment for her family and friends.
Bloomfield Hills, Michigan

A brother-sister team, **Design Ideas**® was formed in 1984 with a million-dollar idea: a wire basket for toting toiletries in college dorms. After early success in the college market, the firm branched out of the bathroom and into the lives of millions of consumers across the U.S. Today, Design Ideas® creates, manufactures, and markets more than 1,700 innovative and affordable accessories for the home and office under the slogan, "We make *things* interesting."
P.O. Box 2967
Springfield, IL 62708
800.426.6394
DesignIdeas@DesignID.com
www.designid.com

Designs by Dorian, a small family business, offer unique customized cake tops for any occasion that are handcrafted to last. The firm specializes in vintage-inspired romantic fantasy cake toppers for weddings, birthdays, anniversaries, or any occasion. Designs by Dorian cake tops are exquisite keepsakes — remembrances of special times.
866.883.1084
Dorian@DesignsbyDorian.com
www.DesignsbyDorian.com

DeVine Corporation is a privately held distributor/wholesaler of fine tableware and giftware to the retail trade in the United States, Canada, Bermuda, and Puerto Rico. Its current product ranges are targeted to better specialty, gift, direct mail, jewelry, tabletop, and gourmet retail environments as well as the upper tier of U.S. department stores. It has a solid reputation for providing quality service and products to a discerning up-market customer base.
1345 Campus Parkway
Neptune, NJ 07753
732. 751.0500

Elaine and Guy Doran, owners of **Doran Greenhouses**, share a great love for incorporating nature with antiques, creating a charming atmosphere. Their settings often draw on their love for Scandinavia, travels, and collectables. *Better Homes and Gardens Magazine* has featured their home twice. Elaine's Christmas collection was photographed as a main source for a popular Christmas collectable book.
150 East St.
Lexington, MA 02420

The Duck Inn, run by Donna Young Whitley, is located on the Currituck Sound in Duck, North Carolina. It offers the perfect getaway.
1158 Duck Road
Duck, NC 27949
252.441.4572
whitleydy@aol.com

Ben Eden is an award-winning fine-art documentary photographer and photojournalist. Based in London, UK, he is available to cover outstanding wedding events and destination weddings worldwide. Ben's approach to wedding photography is simple: He selects his weddings carefully and affords them the same candid, sensitive yet elegant treatment that he applies to his museum-exhibited documentary work.
ben@beneden.com
Ben Eden@BenEden.com

Elegance & Simplicity Wedding & Event Designers, Inc. is the largest event planning and floral design firm in the Washington, DC metropolitan area. In addition to event design, the firm creates daily floral designs and stationery. *Washingtonian Magazine* selected the firm as one of the best wedding planners (Jan. 2005), and *Elegant Bride Magazine* selected it as one of the best florists in the country (Feb./Mar. 2005).
202.625.1470
301.656.5560
800.768.8814
inquiries@eleganceandsimplicity.com
www.eleganceandsimplicity.com
www.dccoutureweddings.com

Fancy Flea Antiques is one of the largest sources for fine porcelains, silver, and estate jewelry in New England.
1841 Massachusetts Ave.
Lexington, MA 02420
781.862. 9650
info@fancyfleaantiques.com
www.fancyfleaantiques.com

Christina Gamota works with strong, bold colors, shapes, and textures. Her settings can be modern, traditional, whimsical, and always detailed. Her ethnic background, and life abroad have left an imprint on her style. Because of her love of design, her homes have appeared in national magazines, such as *Glamour* and *Ladies Home Journal.*
Lexington, MA.

Serving clients in all aspects of floristry, **Grass Roots** specializes in weddings, corporate, and special occasion events. The firm's aim is to make an event both unique and memorable, always using quality floristry to give the best visual impact.
grassrootssb@yahoo.com
www.grassrootssantabarbara.com

Founded in Hungary, in 1826, Herend enjoys a worldwide reputation for quality handcrafted, hand painted porcelain. **Martin's Herend Imports**, a family-owned and operated business, has been the exclusive importer and sole distributor of Herend to the U.S. since 1957. It currently provides Herend to over 400 retail stores nationwide.
800.643.7363
www.herendusa.com.

HudsonValleyWeddings.com is a complete on-line resource for planning a wedding in New York's Hudson Valley. Visitors are offered a free, comprehensive, online Guide & Planner, with new articles added regularly. Brides are "introduced" to hundreds of local vendors providing descriptions and displaying their wedding-related services and products.
120 Morey Hill Rd.
Kingston, NY 12401
845.336.4705
judy@hudsonvalleyweddings.com
http://www.hudsonvalleyweddings.com

Gary Inman, MA, PhD Candidate, Allied Member ASID, is a notable East Coast design talent. In his role as president and principal designer of Gary Inman Interiors, Ltd, a Virginia-based firm, Inman combines elements from the past with the best of contemporary design to create livable, sophisticated spaces. Inman maintains an active lecture schedule for museums as well as TV programs; has been a featured columnist for *Richmond Magazine* and *Chesapeake Home*, and been dubbed "a true Renaissance man."
3215 Monument Ave.
Richmond, VA 23221
804.358.7506
palladio@erols.com
www.garyinman.com

Kate Dickerson, owner of **Kate Dickerson Design, Inc.**, is an interior designer with a passion for rich colors, elegant textures, and unusual pairings of fabrics and accessories. Her flair for "Classic European styling…*with Pizzazz*" informs her interiors as well as her table settings. Her boutique in Hingham Square, Massachusetts, is stocked with fabrics, furniture, china, crystal, and tabletop accessories.

132 North St.
Hingham Square, MA 02043
781.749.8808
kate@katedickerson.com
www.katedickerson.com

Katering by Kim is the Outer Banks premier caterer, designing ceremony into reception, matching personalities with style, managing lighting, linens, florals, menu, cake, colors, and more. Chef Louis Petrozza is a graduate of The Culinary Institute of America, with 20 years of experience
252.441.7010
info@kateringbykim.com
www.kateringbykim.com

Founded in 1876, **Lexington Field and Garden Club** is a dedicated group of women and men who share a common interest and love of gardening. The club's interests take many forms, from vegetable gardening, to traffic island maintenance, civic improvement, floral design, and all garden-related things in between. Members are residents of Lexington, Massachusetts, and more than 14 other surrounding towns.
www.lexgardenclub.org

Lexington Historical Society is responsible for acquiring, maintaining, and preserving the significant historical landmarks, artifacts, and archival material of this historic town. The activities of the society are supported by its members, visitors, donations, and bequests from individuals and institutions.
P.O. Box 514
Lexington, MA 02421
781.862.1703
info@lexingtonhistory.org

Tuulikki Loring's work is characterized by warmth, charm, color, and idiosyncratic choice. In business since 1985, she had designed both contemporary and traditional interiors. Her strength is her Finnish heritage, her use of design and color, and her combinations of antiques with contemporary china and glassware.
33 Bloomfield St.
Lexington, MA 02421
781. 862.4672
tuulikki@rcn.com

Luminex is an innovative fabric that emits light. It can be used for various products, including tablecloths.
LUMINEX S.P.A.
Via dei Fossi 14/b
59100 Prato, Italy
39 (0) 57 473 02 83
www.luminex.it

A living example of Swiss hotel tradition at its very best, **Mandarin Oriental Hotel du Rhône** has a superb location on the River Rhône, sitting within the heart of Geneva's business, shopping, and historic district. Unparalleled service and luxury make it the ideal choice for discerning business and leisure travelers.
Quai Turrettini
1201 Geneva, Switzerland
41 (0) 22 909 00 00
mogva-reservations@mohg.com
www.mandarinoriental.com/geneva

Marked for Dessert is Chicago's most distinctive cake boutique, created by pastry chef and cake stylist Mark Seaman. It specializes in elegant wedding cakes with handmade sugar flowers of life-like gum paste and beautiful pulled sugar. The firm can design a unique cake for any special event.
1812 W. Greenleaf
Chicago, IL 60626
773.761.3800
info@markedfordessert.com
www.markedfordessert.com

Christel McCarthy is a collector of anything that strikes her fancy. Her decorating shows her love for American antiques and color. A trained landscape decorator, she composes elegant palettes of color, shape, and structure.
Lexington, MA

A leading wedding planning agency in France, **Piece Montee** can provide you with its tailor-made services. The company organizes any type of celebrations and receptions in the most beautiful French settings: Paris, Loire Valley, and South of France. The clients particularly enjoy ceremonies in historical venues, in the park of a chateau, on private beaches, on a boat facing the Eiffel Tower, in Montmartre, and in many other exciting venues.
83 rue de Turbigo,
75 003 Paris, France
33 1 44 59 67 17
celine@piecemontee.com
www.piecemontee.com

Rhodec International design was created by Donne Booysen, Kelly Garcia, Martina MacGreevy, Claire Pryce, Juliet Racoosin, and Fiona Worboys. Rhodec International is a distance-learning college for interior design, offering diplomas and bachelor degrees. The American Society of Interior Designers (ASID), the International Interior Design Association (IIDA), and the National Council for Interior Design Qualification (NCIDQ) all recognize their certificates as professional standard.

59 Coddington St., Suite 104,
Quincy, MA 02169
617.472.4942
uscontact@rhodec.edu

One of the largest furniture manufacturers in the United States, **Stanley Furniture Co., Inc.** is widely recognized as a style and design leader. The company has received ten coveted Pinnacle Awards for fine quality residential wood furniture, ranging from traditional to contemporary. Stanley Furniture collections are presented as dining room, bedroom, home entertainment and accent tables, and home office.
276.627.2000
stanleyfurniture.com

Stelle Events specializes in coordinating events in the greater California Bay Area and for Americans in Italy. Stelle Events provides the highest level of service, including travel arrangements, accommodations, event sites, caterers, florists, photographers, transportation, hair and make up artists, favors, daily itineraries for guests, and pre-event information such as detailed maps, save the date cards, and invitations.
47 Marin Bay Park Ct.
San Rafael, CA 94901
415.218.8223
info@stelleevents.com
www.stelleevents.com

Siobhan Theriault is a dynamic photographer whose sense of humor radiates in her pictures of animals and children. Her still-lifes are characterized by sensitivity and charm.
Bedford, MA

A former New York fashion editor and stylist, **Mary Lou Touart** is currently a newspaper columnist. Her abiding interest in fashion includes parallel interests in interior design and architecture. She brings her knowledge, sense of humor, and discriminating taste to bear on her innovative decorating.
Lexington, MA

Tricia Traxler takes on decorating and painting projects through her firm, **Tricia Traxler Interiors, Interior Design and Re-Design**. With a pronounced European, old-world look and feel, Tricia uses color and art to enliven her projects. Her whimsical collections make their way to the table to create theme dinners, parties, and get-togethers. She also consults on garden design and relishes the opportunity to blur the lines between home and garden by bringing garden objects inside.
Winchester, MA
781.721.2489
ttraxler@comcast.net

Index